PRAISE AND LOVE
FOR HAPPY AND FREE ON PURPOSE

What a wonderful book Lauren G. Foster has written! I've been waiting for someone to put all the lovely, pragmatic, and insightful things I've learned over the past 40 years in one place— and here it is. Lauren is a master craftsman—crafting a book that leads us very gently and with amazing stories and exercises to a place that assures revitalization, aligned purpose, and meaningful activities. In very short order, she leads the way to creating a life that flows with happiness, growth, and fulfillment. Whether you are finding these lessons for the first time, or want succinct reminders, the lessons are clearly and newly relevant as we each commit to our new normal. I especially loved the "Magic Orchid" exercise. I'm sure you will too!"
~ *Karen Flaherty, Living by Human Design*

Happy and Free On Purpose is an enjoyably paced and accessible primer on the Law of Attraction. If you're already a Law of Attraction fan, this will be a welcome review. If you're new to the material, Foster provides a solid introduction. The summary at the end with proposed exercises that you could do with a book club or accountability group is particularly helpful. My favorite takeaway and a good summary of the essence of this book are the authors' words: "Happiness is not something you find. I finally let life teach me that happiness is something you choose, create, and generate."
~ *Caroline Ceniza-Levine, DreamCareerClub.com*

"I have read other books on joy, but never finished them. Lauren's book kept my attention, and I was hooked. If you are someone who is still chasing 'Happiness' STOP and read this book. I love the format, encouragement, and exercises. I read through it once and will read it again in more detail and have a lot of fun with it. And then read it again! (There should be a part two). This will make a wonderful gift to self, family, and friends.
~ *Cindy Fay Lybbert, Master PSYCH-K Facilitator*

Lauren Foster's happiness is infectious, and her book shows that any of us can live that way. It's full of practical steps we can take now from right where we are. I especially loved her ideas for a morning ritual, to start each day in joy. This book puts happiness within anyone's reach—talk about empowering!
~ *Shani Fox, ND - Physician, Coach, Cancer Survivorship Expert*

Interested in mastering the art of manifestation, while learning how to love your life more than you ever thought possible? This is your guide. Lauren Foster takes you step by step through the process of discovering what blocks you from the life you dream of having and paves the way in doable, intuitive, and comprehensive steps. This book is my new favorite reading to remind me how to get back on track with the business of living my best life. If you have a craving to understand yourself and your relationship to what you manifest in your life, drop what you're doing and read this book now. It delivers.
~ *Nora Yolles Young, BCH – Young Hypnotherapy*

This book is filled with wisdom, but also very practical, which is what I love most when reading a great book. I want to put the words into actions and see the results unfold in my life. The power of our thoughts is incredible, and we can manifest the life we want. Even if this is a topic I teach myself, Lauren breaks this massive subject down into small actionable chunks so that everyone, regardless of how much or how little you have already learned, will reach a new level after doing the exercises she guides us through. "We are all spiritual beings having a human experience." This is not a book to read once, but a guide to keep on your journey and pick up again and again.

~ Rachel Smets, Clarity Coach, Freedom Lifestyle creator.

Happy and Free
On Purpose

LEARN DAILY PRACTICES TO LIVE AND LOVE YOUR LIFE!

Lauren G. Foster

Happy and Free On Purpose
Learn Daily Practices to Live and Love Your Life!

Copyright © 2021

All rights reserved. No part of this book may be reproduced by any method for public or private use–other than for "fair use" as brief quotations embodied in articles and reviews–without prior written permission of the publisher.

The intent of the author is to provide general information to individuals who are taking positive steps in their lives for personal, emotional and spiritual well-being. If you use any of the information in this book for yourself, the author and the publisher assume no responsibility for your actions. Readers are encouraged to seek the counsel of competent professionals with regards to such matters.

Powerful You! Publishing is committed to publishing works of quality and integrity. In that spirit, we are proud to offer this book to our readers; however, the story, the experiences, and the words are the author's alone.

Published by: Powerful You! Inc. USA

powerfulyoupublishing.com

Library of Congress Control Number: 2021909904

Lauren G. Foster—First Edition

ISBN: 978-1-7356579-3-6

First Edition July 2021

SELF-HELP / Personal Growth / Happiness

DEDICATION

To Scott:

So much more than family, you've been my best friend and my rock. A million times you said, "write a book, write a book" …. And I finally did, thanks to you! Hopefully it's the first of many. So, I thank you from me and on behalf of all the people that will be uplifted.

Table of Contents

Introduction	xi
Part I ~ Getting Ready To Get Ready	1
Chapter 1 ~ How To Get the Most From This Book	5
Chapter 2~ How I Got Here: A Story of Manifestation	9
Chapter 3 ~ Becoming Aware Of Your Beliefs	19
Chapter 4 ~ Pay Attention To The Words You Speak	25
Part II ~ Learning To Create Our Life On Purpose	27
Chapter 5 ~ What Do You Already Love About Your Life?	31
Chapter 6 ~ What Do You Most Want To Change?	39
Chapter 7~ Rediscover Lost Parts Of Yourself	45
Chapter 8~ Wishes Unfulfilled	51
Chapter 9 ~Get In Touch With Your Values	55
Chapter 10~ Inventory Your Toolbox	61
Chapter 11 ~ Identify Your Passions	65
Part III ~ Creating A New Story	67
Chapter 12 ~ Write The New Story Of Your Dream Life	71
Chapter 13 ~ Test Your New Story. Is It Worthy Of You?	81
Part IV ~ New Ways Of "Being", Living, And Creating Your New Life	83
Chapter 14 ~ Magnificent Manifesting Mornings	87

Part V ~ Specific Focus On General Areas Of Your Life	101
Chapter 15 ~ Be In Love With Your Body	105
Chapter 16 ~ Fall Back In Love With Love And Your Your Loved Ones	121
Chapter 17 ~ For The Love Of Money	129
Chapter 18 ~ Loving Your Space And Your Daily Life	135
Part VI ~ Putting It All Together	143
Chapter 19 ~ Three Common Obstacles And Challenges	147
Chapter 20 ~ Study And Practice Guide	155
Resources	163
Note From The Author	167

INTRODUCTION

What does it mean to be happy and free on purpose? It means that you *know* you get to choose and you *use* that power. You live where you want to live, do work you love to do and generate money in the amounts you want. You feel great in your body, connected and in touch and knowing the right things to do to maximize your health, beauty, and vitality. You are moving forward through inspired action, totally in love with your life right now, and completely excited about the great things to come.

You have the gift of recognizing and reveling in small things. You watch with awe and delight as the world seems to line up for you, you see the evidence that things are always working out for your good. You feel loved and supported and connected to your source.

You want everything you want—the loving relationship, fulfilling work, abundant money, vibrant health, and the freedom to do and be and create in any way you like—because you think you will be happier when you have it. The great news is that you never have to wait for these things—you can be happy now! You can learn how to choose happiness first, and then just watch as your desires start to show up in your life.

It's good to want things. It's part of your purpose to keep expanding and growing and becoming a better and better version of yourself. Your purpose is joy, so embrace it and start choosing it, today!

This book will teach you how to fall in love with your life as it currently is *and* be in love with the dreams you are creating. There is ALWAYS a "bright" side, and with practice you will learn to find it easily and automatically.

PART I
GETTING READY TO GET READY

"If a man knows not to which port he sails, no wind is favorable." ~ Seneca

Every great journey starts with some preparation. There is great joy and satisfaction in making a plan, in being deliberate and gathering together the tools and toys you need to have a fantastic experience. I imagine this section is like getting ready for a new schoolyear, with fresh clean notebooks, pens and pencils, folders, and binders. (I LOVE office supplies!) You may envision yourself going on a wonderful trip, gathering the things you want to wear, gifts for people you'll visit, maybe new luggage or sleepwear. This section is all about setting yourself up for success, so make up your mind right now that this is going to be fun! Decide that learning and getting back in touch with who you really are will be the best time of your life!

"You can't get it wrong, and you'll never get it done."

- Abraham Hicks

CHAPTER 1
HOW TO GET THE MOST FROM THIS BOOK

This book is the first step of a journey, one in which you take note of—and start appreciating—where you currently are, get in touch with yourself and figure out what you would really love, and then apply daily practices to LIVE that life, loving every minute in joyful anticipation of what comes next. This is simple, but it's not easy. You must honor your decision to be the deliberate creator of your life and give your journey the attention it needs and deserves.

It took me many years to figure this out, and more years to fully utilize these life skills to manifest my life in the way I wanted. I'm still on this path and always will be—creating new dreams and visions and new ways of being present and in love with the present moment. My hope is that you can skip all that trial and error and get right to the good stuff—choosing happiness and freedom every day.

I recommend that you first read this book in its entirety so you can plant seeds in your subconscious before coming back and really working through each chapter for yourself or with your group. Chapter 15 is a step-by-step study guide that corresponds with all of the different sections. I also suggest that you get a journal. This will be your life planner and your best friend on your journey to happiness and freedom, so make it important, make it special, and make it sacred! I'll share a couple of my favorites in the Resources section at the end.

Before we get started, I want to share a little bit about my story so you know where I'm coming from and how I put these principles in action to create a life that I love.

"Do what you can, with what you have, where you are."

— Theodore Roosevelt

CHAPTER 2
HOW I GOT HERE: A STORY OF MANIFESTATION

I discovered at a very young age what it means to be free and find my own way. As the youngest of six kids I was often left to my own devices while my mother was busy dealing with my five older siblings. The flipside of that freedom is that I got into some trouble that I might otherwise have been protected from: molestation, exposure to drugs and alcohol way too early, injuries and accidents, and getting beaten up by school bullies. Fortunately, I figured out pretty early that those traumas and dramas can only be the guiding force in my life if I let them. I somehow got the message that all of my experiences, good and bad, had molded me into the person I was, and I tried really hard to like that person. I could be a "victim," keeping active all of the things that had gone wrong, or I could forge ahead and try to make new choices.

I was a very religious adolescent, spending a lot of my time in church and pledging my life to missionary service when I was just thirteen. I loved the Minister of Youth and Music and his sweet, beautiful wife, and I loved the creative outlet singing and acting in church plays provided me. Best of all, I felt safe and secure within the fold of a loving church family.

An unfortunate series of events would rip that safety net right out from under me. First, our youth minister went to

Brazil to do missionary work. Then our pastor got caught in an indiscretion with a parishioner. As if this wasn't bad enough, a criminal set fire to the church to create a distraction so she could break her boyfriend out of jail! Just like that, my church foundation had gone up in smoke. When services resumed, the new leadership didn't resonate with me. Instead of messages of love and acceptance, I now heard things like, "Be careful with your eye makeup. Your eyes are provocative and might make men think sinful thoughts." I was also supposed to give "hugs from the side," lest I make contact with my breasts and incite lust. Realizing it was no longer the church I knew and loved, my attachment to it faded away, but my love of service and my instinctual connection to God and spirit remained.

This foundation, along with the unconditional love of my family and the lessons born of all that early freedom, gave me the courage to go out and make life happen on my own terms. And I did! I am fifty-five, and at last count I've had thirty-seven jobs and moved twenty-one times. There were about sixteen relationships, including one marriage and divorce, not counting one night stands. I stopped screwing around and finally finished college; I created careers and tanked them. I did some traveling, saw some things, and had a lot of fun. Yet I was always *chasing* happiness, never realizing that no matter where I went, I was taking my restless spirit and seeking heart with me.

I had always done well financially, well enough that I was the one my family came to for support. As a professional salesperson, I'd been taught to visualize successful outcomes and have high energy. I was also a student of positive psychology, the Law of Attraction, spirituality, and the power of the mind over matter. I thought I was a really good little manifester,

Chapter 2 - How I Got Here: A Story Of Manifestation

getting things done, taking care of everybody else, full of ego and pride. So I earned and I gave. I succeeded and I fell down. I always got back up, started over, and always landed on my feet...until the day I didn't.

In 2007 I had an accidental pregnancy, and not with the right guy (I forgot to even count him in the sixteen!). But it was a happy accident—I was forty-three-years old and had thought my childbearing years were behind me. Then the doctor gave me the devastating news—the fetus had not attached and I was going to miscarry. That was the beginning of my biggest downward spiral. I lost my cushy, high-paying job and decided to liquidate everything and take a sabbatical. I spent about six months in Guatemala and traveling a bit in Europe before the call of family brought me back to the States.

By that time it was late 2008 and, unbeknownst to me, the US economy had completely tanked. I bought a one-third interest in my favorite day spa, with no research, no service industry experience, no training or licensing to allow me to "work" in my own business. By 2010, I was bankrupt, jobless, and homeless, camped out in my sister's spare room. Temping at the local radio and TV stations, housesitting, and taking other odd jobs gave me just enough to keep me in wine and cigarettes. This was my lowest point. I had nothing, I didn't want to try to get back up, because I'd probably just have to give whatever I had to my family, or maybe I'd lose it all again.

The blows just kept coming. My brother died; my mom had to be moved to a state-run nursing home because no one had the money to pay for a better place. I had completely exhausted myself financially, emotionally, and physically, with nothing to show for it. For all of my attempts to create in the reality of others, I had, in the end, helped no one. Had my sister been in a position to support me, I could have easily lived out the rest of my life just like that: aimless, purposeless, numbed by alcohol and casual sex, neither knowing nor caring what came next. But she was in an even worse place than me, and about to lose her home. As my apathy didn't extend to being on-the-streets homeless, I was forced to dig deep for the will to once again find some purpose and joy in life.

From this humble place, I realized that I wasn't anyone's hero, nor was I meant to be. Everyone has their own path and the same access to the Universe as I do; it wasn't my job to take care of them. I handed my mom, my sisters and brothers, and my beloved nephew over to God, put my blinders on, and headed in the direction of what I wanted.

All those years of studying spirituality, positive psychology, and the Law of Attraction had provided me with a ton of life skills. So I pulled them all out and from the simplest of places began to rebuild my life. I didn't envision mansions and millions of dollars, fame and fortune. I created a simple dream. I wanted work that came easy to me and gave me the freedom to create my own schedule and not cap my income. I wanted a little piece of land and a small house that was very isolated. I wanted to have the freedom to have doors and windows open all the time and for my dog and cats and me to be free and safe. I wanted a place in which I could hunker down and heal and create, in solitude, serenity, silence, and peace.

Once I got clear on what I wanted and planted the vision of how that would feel in my mind, things started to happen very quickly. With one phone call, I found a position as an independent contractor in advertising sales, with a product that was very reputable and pretty easy to sell. I could live anywhere and work from home. They were willing to pay a stipend to help me while I built the business. They wanted a specific end result but had no desire to dictate how I got there. I was completely free to work my way, to make my own schedule, and create my own business. It's important to note that this type of arrangement was exactly what they wanted as well, and that I had known about this opportunity for a year. I just couldn't see it because I had been assuming many things—that I would be micromanaged, that they would be demanding and make me adhere to a schedule, or show up at an office. NONE of this was true and it was a perfect match.

Next, I found an area in beautiful East Tennessee, where there was a lot of the kind of property I wanted. My sister's house had finally been foreclosed on, and I was not yet in a position to purchase anything, so I found a basement apartment that I could afford and was near where I wanted to buy. It was tiny—just two hundred-fifty square feet for me, my dog, and four cats—but it was nice to have my own place again. I did my work and took my dog on lots of hikes, exploring the area and looking at every property that matched my dream. I also started searching for a bank that would finance me despite a brand-new bankruptcy. Most importantly, I kept my eyes on the dream and my heart in the most grateful place I could find. I made lists of positive aspects of the tiny little apartment that was my home. I praised my healthy body and my sweet pets, and my friends. Every day, I DECIDED that I would be in love with my life and that I would be excited, expectant, and have total faith that my dream home was coming, very soon.

I found a place I thought was perfect, but I could not secure financing for it yet and the owner didn't offer any other options. This troubled me NOT ONE BIT, as I knew this just meant that another, even better place was on the way. In the meantime, I stayed grateful, and I learned for myself that happiness is not something you *find*. I finally let life teach me that happiness is something you *choose*, create, and generate. I learned that when I was focused on the neighbor's loud music or my freezing apartment, I felt crappy. But when I focused on the little screened-in porch with the view of the lake, or pizza delivery, or the beauty all around me, I was happy. No amount of learning and studying could measure up to what I proved to myself. You can be happy anywhere, in any situation. It just depends on where you put your attention.

One year later, I found *the* perfect place nestled in the mountains on five acres. It was a fairy cottage on the outside and a log cabin on the inside, with an open floorplan, high vaulted ceiling, and a sweet little loft bedroom. There were no neighbors to speak of, and it was completely safe, silent, serene, and lovely. It was exactly what I had envisioned, better than and half the price of the one I'd wanted and couldn't get. I still couldn't get financing, but the owner agreed to rent it to me until my bankruptcy aged one more year. And that's exactly what happened. The following year I was the owner of my dream home. I built a series of decks outside where I worked and played with my dog and cats. Long lovely hikes and picnics at lunch on my very own mountain became my reality. I was thriving!

It was there, sitting at my sweet little patio table with my dog at my feet, completely in love with my life, that I realized that THIS is my purpose! I wanted to teach other women how to achieve this kind of happiness and spare them the ups and downs and spectacular failures of my own journey. I dubbed myself a "Happiness Coach" (I thought I made up that term!) and Be Happy First was born!

Now I have a new dream: a lodge and retreat center right here in these amazing mountains, where I can host meditation retreats and introduce people to the joys of wandering around in a temperate rainforest. I want another retreat in a tropical location—maybe on the beach or on Lake Atitlan in Guatemala, a place I fell in love with. I love my life and I am so excited and expectant of the amazing things that are coming next. I love dreaming and watching those dreams manifest. I love figuring out ways to get this message to the women who are really yearning for and ready for it. Happiness is a choice! Learn how to choose happiness! Be Happy First and everything else will fall into place in perfect time.

Ready to get started? I have total faith in you and I KNOW that your life is unfolding perfectly. The Universe has your back and so do I! Welcome to your journey. Get ready to be happy and free!

"Whether you think you can or you think you can't - you're right."

- Henry Ford

CHAPTER 3
BECOMING AWARE OF YOUR BELIEFS

The prevailing theme throughout and behind every word of this book is this: if you believe it, it's true. For you. Our lives are largely lived automatically, from patterns already implanted in our subconscious. Right or wrong, true or false, if your subconscious believes something to be true, then that becomes your reality. We are not going to go back through your life and examine everything that happened to you, identify traumas, or find out when, why, or how you got these beliefs. We're just going to notice them when they affect our present, flush them out, and replace them with new beliefs. Beliefs that serve you.

If for whatever reason you feel unworthy or undeserving, we will replace those beliefs with the absolute truth of your divinity. You are precious, unique, and eternal, deserving and worthy of all things, just because you exist. Your life on this earth is a gift, no strings attached, from a Universe that loves you unconditionally, no matter what, and wants you to thrive and expand and experience all that this human journey has to offer. You weren't put here casually or by accident. You have a unique purpose and you will find your greatest joy when you let go of expectations and trying to please others and begin to live according to your own unique purpose. Happy and Free

ON PURPOSE, has a double meaning. It means that you are deliberate and intentional, like when your little brother shouted, "She did that on purpose!" It also means that you are living according to YOUR purpose—on your path, in love with the present moment, and bright-eyed, curious, and excited about the surprises and adventures that lie ahead.

In every category that we explore in this book, be it health, money, relationships, or everyday joy and fulfillment, we will take time to examine your beliefs. If you believe that being healthy and fit means hard work, deprivation, and misery, this will be your truth. If any part of you believes in the "no pain, no gain" philosophy created by the fitness industry, make up your mind that this is not a belief that serves you and get to work creating a new belief. "Me and my body are best friends and we know just how to eat and move and live to have the most joyous and alive experience imaginable" is a much more empowering belief. Life is supposed to be fun. Life is supposed to be joyous. No matter what your path, your purpose is joy. If you believe having money is bad, you will never attract money. If you think the only way to be prosperous is to sacrifice all of your time and joy, that will be your experience. If you believe that you aren't good enough, smart enough, pretty enough, or anything else enough to deserve an amazing life, this will be your reality. This book will teach you how to BECOME the person you really are, to get in touch with the highest parts of yourself, and train your brain to believe in the amazingness of YOU!

The way to replacing limiting beliefs with empowering ones is simple. Again, we are not going to try to undo or heal or dissect your past experiences. Instead, we will wash them away by flooding your mind and soul with positive new beliefs.

Beliefs that serve you. Beliefs that lift you up and add joy to every moment of your life.

As you're reading and working through the activities, notice when doubt, skepticism, and that critical little voice inside of you show up. This is the voice that asks, "Who are you to think that you could _____?" This question is valuable, for it clues you in to a limiting belief that can be reframed and reprogrammed.

Start now to become aware. Start noticing and paying attention to the thoughts and feelings that emerge for you. Get to know yourself and identify your own patterns, on the way to learning a new way to talk to yourself. Having unconditional love for the preciousness of you will catapult you toward fantastic joy and satisfaction faster than anything. Your emotions are your own personal GPS system. Make feeling good your number one priority!

"Be impeccable with your word."
- Don Miguel Ruiz

CHAPTER 4
PAY ATTENTION TO THE WORDS YOU SPEAK

I love and highly recommend the book *The Four Agreements* by Don Miguel Ruiz. The statement on the previous page—Be impeccable with your word—is the first and most important agreement, as it's the one the other three flow from. Words have power! They tell you what you are thinking and what your beliefs are, and they have the power to create.

Your thoughts really do become things. They manifest first as feelings, then as words and actions that eventually appear in your outer reality. The words you speak are a great clue to the thoughts you think. "I *can't do* this because I *have to* do that" is the most disempowering statement in the English language. First, there is nothing you "can't" do. Maybe you won't, maybe you don't want to, maybe you choose not to, but you can. Anything you want to do, there is a way to do it. Any question you have, the Universe has an answer to. There is also nothing that you "have to" do. You might not like the consequences of not doing something, or feel obligated, but you don't have to. Just this simple rewording will give you back your power: "I am *not going* to do this because I *choose* to do that." How simple. Understanding that you are the master of your destiny, that you choose to, want to, are going to, or GET to do whatever you choose to do will shift your thinking in amazing ways!

I love the example of changing "I have to pick up my kids from school" to "I GET to pick up my kids from school." You chose those kids and you love them and you love your role as a mother. You are a master of your life so that you can be available to pick them up from school, hear about their day, and spend time with them. How much more amazing is the feeling that you are empowered to make this choice, rather than feeling that you "have to"?

If "I can't afford that" is a common phrase for you, you will never be able to have all the things you want. Instead say, "That isn't in the budget at this time." Also, if you are in the habit of thinking that you have to sacrifice one thing for another, as in "I can *either* have money *or* I can have love," change those thoughts to, "I can have financial success AND love." Remember, never either/or. Always YES/AND!

Pay attention to the words you say and look for the clues they are giving you about your thoughts. Please learn to speak kindly and gently to and about yourself. I AM is the most powerful phrase there is, so always be sure that the words that follow are kind and positive. I often hear people I dearly love say terrible things about themselves. "I am a train wreck."; "I am a hot mess."; "I am fat,stupid, ugly" .... Breaks my heart. You ARE divine, perfect, precious, and eternal. You are not your body. You are not your diagnosis. You are not your race, religion, or sexual orientation. You HAVE these things. You have a body; you have a diagnosis of whatever. When you notice yourself giving away your power with your words, stop and make a new choice.

PART II
LEARNING TO CREATE YOUR LIFE ON PURPOSE

"If you can tune into your purpose and really align with it, setting goals so that your vision is an expression of that purpose, then life flows much more easily." ~Jack Canfield

Congratulations! You have taken the first step on a beautiful journey to being the best version of yourself and living your best life. In the previous section you learned that you see what you're looking for, you get what you expect, and you attract what you ARE. You also learned the power of your thoughts and words in creating your reality, and saw how I used this power to completely change my life. In this section we'll get into how you can choose happiness to manifest your own desires. If I can do it, so can you, so it's time to get excited about what comes next!

"Dwell on the beauty of life. Watch the stars and see yourself running with them."

– Marcus Aurelius

CHAPTER 5
WHAT DO YOU ALREADY LOVE ABOUT YOUR LIFE?

You are where you are. There is not one thing you can do about that; you can't go back and start over and you can't leap ahead to where you want to be. The great news is that where you are is the EXACT perfect place. In this moment lies all of your power, so make peace with it, feel all the joy that is available to you, and embrace the divinity that is you.

Remember, your mission is to shift your perspective so you are totally in love with this moment and eagerly anticipating the wonders that are in store for you. How do you do this? By setting the intention, right now, to change the way you look at life. Start looking for aspects to appreciate instead of things to complain about. Look for what is pleasing instead of what is not. No matter what is happening in your life that is not to your liking, there are many things that ARE to your liking. Start teaching yourself right now to look for those things, and to cultivate feelings of joy, appreciation, and love for everything that is currently present. (Don't worry, you'll have a short window of time to complain in just a few pages.) When you place your attention on the good things in your life, you'll soon find more of them showing up with shocking frequency.

WHAT DO YOU LOVE ABOUT YOUR BODY?

It can be easy to focus on what's wrong when we are experiencing illness or dis-ease in some part of the body. One way to shift this is to recognize that despite this, there are still thousands of processes happening perfectly. Your body is amazing and deserves your praise and appreciation, no matter what. Look at and love all of the parts of your body that are awesome and don't let your diagnosis become the star of your show. Later on, we'll talk about what messages your body is trying to send to you through your pain or dis-ease. You'll learn how to tune in and listen and become best friends with your body.

WHAT CAN YOU APPRECIATE ABOUT YOUR FINANCES RIGHT NOW?

One of the things people struggle with most is financial abundance. If you don't yet have all of the money you want, the key is to shift your focus to what you do have. This can be the roof over your head, the food you ate today, your clothes, or even the money you had to buy this book. When you look at your life through this lens, you'll find many material things to appreciate while you begin learning how to manifest more abundance.

WHAT ARE THE ENDEARING AND LOVABLE ASPECTS OF YOUR PEOPLE?

Even the most challenging people in your life have bright, shining aspects. If your relationships are not bringing you joy, take some time to remind yourself how much you love these people and all the reasons why. Instead of looking at your differences and the ways they "make" you feel, look for the parts of them that are endearing and lovable.

WHAT CAN YOU CHOOSE TO LOVE ABOUT YOUR WORK?

If you hate your job, the commute, your boss, your coworkers, your paycheck, et cetera, know that you can start changing it right now. The first step is to make peace with where you currently are, bring your finest self into every situation, and cultivate gratitude for each aspect of your work life (i.e. any tasks that you do enjoy, positive aspects of your colleagues, or the things your paycheck does allow you to afford). In doing so, you will be building an incredible jumping off place to create something new.

WHAT ARE THE BEAUTIFUL QUALITIES OF YOUR HOME?

Don't like where you live? You can change that too, again, by training your mind to focus on what you do love. No matter how crappy your neighbors are, how icky the weather, how leaky the roof, I know you can find aspects of your current home that are great. Perhaps it is the proximity to a lovely park, or your favorite piece of furniture. Choose to amplify those.

WHAT DO YOU LOVE ABOUT YOUR LIFESTYLE?

Do you have traditions with friends and family that nurture you? Do you regularly lunch with friends or travel or spend a day at the spa? Do you enjoy long baths and afternoons curled up with a book? Do you have fun projects that you do by yourself or with people you love? Do you host or attend dinner parties or book clubs or tea parties? What is awesome about your daily life right now?

Use your attention to magnify the positive aspects of every part of your life and watch the negative aspects wither and die from neglect.

Here is a fun exercise. Before you turn the page, set a timer for ten seconds. Turn the page, start the timer, and count all of the squares on the page. After ten seconds, write down your answer.

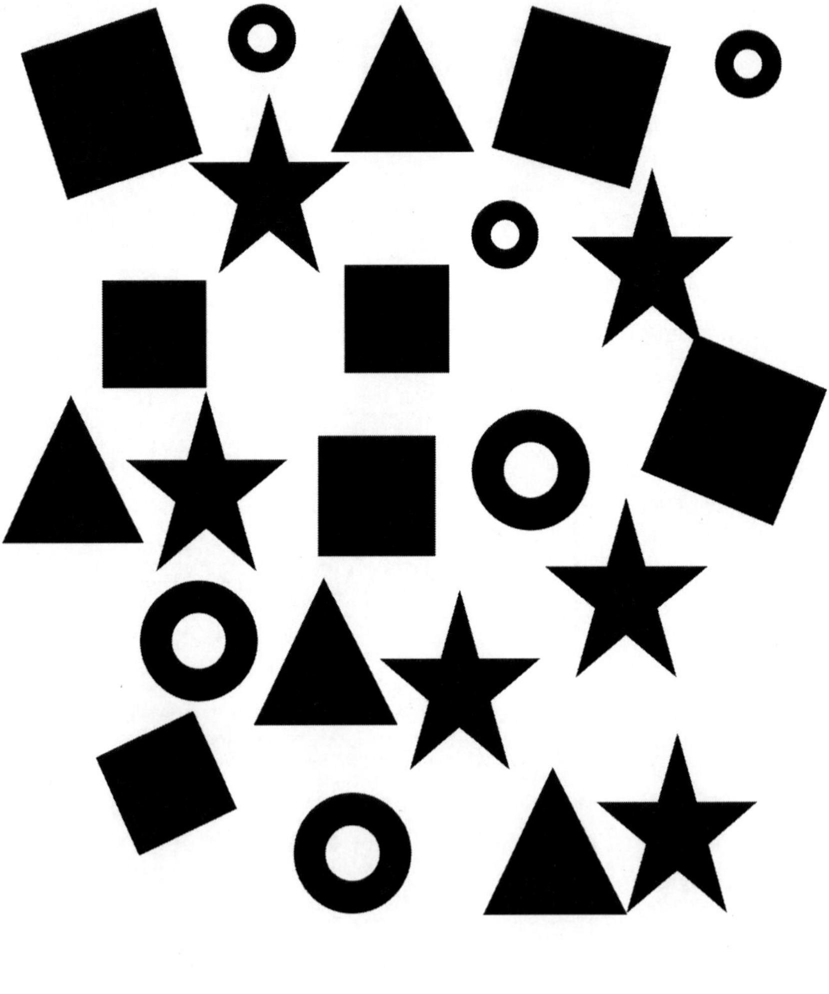

Did you get seven? If so, you're right! Now, without looking again, how many stars? Don't know, right? (Unless you're one of the rare people that counted everything or has a photographic memory) That's because you weren't LOOKING for stars! You found squares because that's what you were looking for and that's exactly how life works! If you are seeking and counting up bright shiny things, that is your reality. If you're looking for dark, stormy, unhappy events and things to complain about, that is your reality too. The great news is that you get to choose; in fact, you are already doing so, even when you don't realize it. In every moment you are choosing where you put your attention, what you are looking for, and what you expect.

Take some time to make lists of everything you can think of to love and appreciate about each of these areas of your life. Be sure to leave room to come back and add more as you become more positive and better at seeing the good. This is your life you're creating, so treat it with reverence and love. (Your beautiful journal is a sacred place for doing this most important work.)

You're off to a great start! Great work!

"If you want something you've never had, you must be willing to do something you've never done."

– Thomas Jefferson

CHAPTER 6
WHAT DO YOU MOST WANT TO CHANGE?

When you know what you don't want, you get great clues about what you DO want. That's why in this chapter (and ONLY this chapter) we'll spend some time looking at the negative.

There's a good chance that you picked up this book because you are really unhappy—maybe even at your wits' end—and ready to try anything to feel better. I hope not. I hope you just have a knowing that life has more to offer than what you've currently manifested. The truth is, though, that human beings often have to hit "rock bottom" before they are willing and able to look for help, try new things, and take action to try to feel better. They don't address their health until they are diagnosed with an illness or are in unbearable pain, or the devastation of a broken heart sends them to the self-help section of the bookstore. Remember my story? I didn't get things really figured out until I was completely lost and starting over from nothing.

It doesn't matter how you got here; all that matters is that you are. So if you're in a lot of pain right now, say thank you, because that pain was the catalyst to help you launch the next best version of your life. It's a gift. You're in the right place. You're not alone. I promise that if you follow the path laid out in this book, get to know yourself and what you really want, and take the steps to live each day on purpose, you will soon feel better and see the world start to open up for you.

First, you must determine your starting point. It's a little like using your GPS or google maps—usually they know your current location but sometimes you have to input it yourself. That's what we're going to do: take an honest look at your life as it is now. What would you love to improve? Where is there room to grow and learn?

Don't spend a lot of time on this! You don't want to get mired down in the story of how things ARE (from a negative standpoint); you just want to give yourself a starting point, something to measure by. And after you learn what you need to from this exercise, you're not going to look back at it, except maybe in occasional celebration of how far you've come. Remember, you are creating your future, not trying to go back and fix your past.

Now, look at all of the areas of your life and write an honest assessment of how each looks and feels, what you would like to change or improve, what your struggles are, and how you feel about your ability to make changes. This is where you may really see some of the limiting beliefs that we talked about earlier start to come up.

WHAT COULD BE GOING BETTER WITH YOUR BODY?

Take some time to write a summary of your current level of health, fitness, and confidence regarding the earth-suit you're walking around in. List any ailments, dis-ease, dis-comforts, and struggles. How is your self-image? Are you self-conscious about being seen naked or spend a lot of time trying to disguise your body? How often do you criticize your body, or beat yourself up for all the things you think you should or should not be doing to make it better? Don't dwell, just assess your health and your relationship with your body. Do you feel comfortable giving it whatever it wants? Are you getting good sleep? Having fun and spending time outside? Do you have the energy and strength to do the things you want to do? Do you think or believe that any attempts to improve your health have to be difficult or painful? Have any limiting beliefs about what it means to have a strong healthy body popped into your head? Take note and decide you will replace them with beliefs that serve you.

HOW PLEASED OR DISPLEASED ARE YOU WITH YOUR WORK AND MONEY?

Now, move on to your money and career/job/business. This is pretty self-explanatory. Do you have a good relationship with money, or are you always feeling like you don't have enough or are struggling to earn? Do you love your work or dread it? Do you feel a sense of purpose and fulfillment in the way you create in the world and generate money? What would feel better? Do you have negative feelings toward people who have wealth? Do you believe that the only way to be prosperous is to take advantage of other people or be otherwise "bad"? Do you believe that the only way to have abundance is to sacrifice, struggle, and toil? What limiting beliefs surface for you about money? Write a short summary of your current money story.

HOW HAPPY ARE YOU WITH YOUR MOST IMPORTANT RELATIONSHIPS?

Are you happily single? Miserably married? Lonely and yearning for your soulmate? In harmony with your family, or at odds with them? Describe how you get along with everyone who is important in your life right now. Begin to imagine what it will feel like to have all of these relationships looking exactly like you want them to.

HOW MUCH DO YOU LOVE YOUR LIFE? HOW FREE DO YOU FEEL?

How do you feel about your general lifestyle? Do you feel safe and happy and comfortable in your home? Your neighborhood? Your town and country? Do you have the freedom and initiative to do the things you love to do? Travel? Hobbies? Entertaining? Do you feel good just doing nothing? Do you yearn to go more, do more, experience more? Do you have time to take a long bath, or read a cheesy novel, or go to lunch with friends? Or are you pushed and pulled in different directions all day and fall into bed exhausted at night. How does your "free" time feel?

The first chapters may have been easy for you, but probably not. Most people at this stage in their journey are mired in old habits of thought and unable to answer the question, "What do I really want?" They are so used to complaining and seeing the negative that it takes effort to learn to appreciate and praise. I promise, it gets easier.

The next chapters will help you to get in touch with yourself, remember what you love at the level of your soul, and craft a life that fills you with joy, purpose, and a sense of freedom like never before. You are divine. You are unique. You get to create your life any way you want it and the world has no power to dictate who you get to be. Have fun with this! Life is supposed to be fun!

"For in every adult there resides the child that was, and in every child lies the adult that will be."

– John Connolly

CHAPTER 7
REDISCOVER LOST PARTS OF YOURSELF

When we were little kids, we effortlessly used our imaginations to try on different careers and roles—sometimes becoming a ballerina, an astronaut, and a tiger all in one afternoon! Before too long though, we started getting trained to "be realistic"; "stop daydreaming"; "do your homework and clean your room." Doing what others wanted became more important than being ourselves, and we began to live out the patterns and futures dictated to us by our parents, teachers, preachers, peers, our community, and society at large. That powerful childlike imagination was squelched as we lost touch with our own guidance system and began to believe that we were "supposed" to be a certain way.

You were born knowing who you are, what you love, and how you wanted to live your life. It's time to give yourself permission to return there, to reclaim your personal identity and dharma. The tools that follow will help you to get back in touch with that childlike wonder so you can start creating your own path, completely separate from anything the world seems to be demanding from you, and live happily, free, and on purpose!

As you go through them, keep in mind that "on purpose" has a double meaning. It means to live your own purpose, and to live it deliberately and intentionally. "You did that on purpose!" Why, yes, I did.

REAWAKEN YOUR IMAGINATION AND GET BACK IN TOUCH WITH YOU

Make a list of at least twenty-one things you loved to do throughout your life that you might not do anymore. It may start out slowly, but as the creative juices start to flow you will remember more and more things that you loved. Keep going as long as you like, and if you can come up with more than twenty-one, that's fantastic!

Making this list may bring up emotions around how much you enjoyed these things and why you let go of them; you may also realize for the first time how much you've missed them. It will *definitely* help you remember the way you love to feel (i.e. happiness, contentment, etc.) and what makes your soul thrive.

When I was a little girl I had a very special relationship with a pine tree, the kind with a really straight trunk and branches that seem made for climbing. It was our Christmas tree the year I was born so we grew up together, and by the time I was big enough to climb it was very tall. I would climb as high as possible, make myself comfortable and read books for hours. I loved to be up there when it was windy as the tree swayed and moved and it felt adventurous and thrilling. It was one of my favorite places to be during my childhood.

When I made my list, climbing trees and reading in trees made my list. It took me a while to apply this to my life. Did I really want to climb trees? Maybe. It would certainly be fantastic to have the flexibility and strength of a child again. But when I thought about it more, I identified the *feeling* this experience gave me. I loved the solitude and silence and peace of being high in a tree, safe from everything, completely free to do whatever I wanted. And, since my mom and my house were very close by, there were no feelings of danger or isolation. In other words, I had figured out as a very small person how to have everything I wanted: the separation from the hustle and bustle of life, the ability to connect with nature, and the freedom to return easily to civilization whenever I wanted to.

I have now recreated that feeling in my home. I live in a very secluded area, surrounded by trees and nature and mountains, far from busy roads or crowds of people, but just two miles from an interstate that will take me anywhere I want to go. My home has a loft where I spend a lot of my time, up high, feeling free, safe, and secluded. Identifying and remembering what spoke to my soul as a young girl helped me to get in touch with me, understand a piece of my soul's yearning, and build a life that satisfies that innate desire.

Throughout my life I've also loved playing the piano and singing, doing hot yoga, writing and drawing, riding bikes and horses, spending hours in the bath pampering myself and making myself feel beautiful. I loved traveling and driving fast, laying naked in the sun, swimming and diving... You get the idea.

Have fun remembering your life and getting back in touch with the things you loved. Was it walking alone in the woods, riding scary rollercoasters, being in school plays? Remember all of it, make your list, and keep adding to it whenever you think of something new. Enjoy the feeling of the picture of your true self unfolding in your mind.

"Twenty years from now, you will be more disappointed by the things you didn't do than by the ones you did do. So throw off the bowlines, sail away from the safe harbor. Catch the trade winds in your sails. Explore. Dream. Discover."

- Mark Twain

CHAPTER 8
WISHES UNFULFILLED

Now it's time to create a dream list of the things you have longed to do but never got around to...yet. There's no such thing as death (a topic for another time), but someday you will leave this physical body. When that day comes and you look back at this lifetime, what will you wish you had done? Are there places you want to see? People you want to meet? Goals you want to achieve such as building a business, raising a family, or making an impact on the world? Do you want to be famous or wealthy? Do you want to sing in a band, learn to speak another language, master a skill? Write at least twenty-one things you would love to experience or accomplish in this lifetime. Just making this list will activate the forces of the Universe to begin to propel you in the direction of these wishes. We'll get more specific about ways to really begin having these experiences; for now, use this list to get even more intimate with yourself and your true desires. Again, the goal is to get really clear on what YOU want for YOUR life on YOUR own terms, without taking into account anything you believe the world or other people expect from you. What do YOU want to do?

"Values are like fingerprints. Nobody's are the same, but you leave them all over everything you do."

- Elvis Presley

CHAPTER 9
GET IN TOUCH WITH YOUR VALUES

Make a list of your values. Choose from the following list or make up your own, but write down any that you feel are important to you. Then choose the top five that you consider most important, and rank them in order of importance. There are several benefits to this exercise, the first being that you will get to know yourself better. You will also discover if any of your values are in conflict with another. Let's say, for instance, that your two highest values are Adventure and Family. If you're off seeing and experiencing other places and cultures, you won't have that time to spend with your children or a spouse, especially if that spouse does not share your love of travel. Don't get me wrong, I do teach a "you can have it all" philosophy, but if you are feeling torn and conflicted about what you really want, this can steal your joy and stop your forward momentum. This is a LIMITED list of possible values, so please add your own to the list before choosing and ranking your top five. If you're finding this particularly challenging, Brené Brown has a great section in her book *Dare to Lead* that will help you delve further and get a new perspective on living true to your values.

VALUES

    Family
    Faith
    God
    Adventure
    Freedom
    Happiness
    Community
    Kindness
    Environmental Friendliness
    Health
    Honesty
    Open-mindedness
    Tolerance/acceptance
    Loyalty
    Reliability
    Responsibility
    Love
    Success
    Service
    Enjoyment
    Commitment
    Discipline
    Authenticity
    Animal Kindness

Your values are the chosen focal point, no-matter-what, must-have qualities of an extraordinary and satisfied life. These may change and evolve over time, so look at what is important to you today. My highest value is freedom—such a simple word that says so much. It means I am free to choose everything. I get to choose the work I do, the life I live, the thoughts I think, the feelings I feel, what I do with my body, how I "worship," how I earn and spend money, who I hang around with… EVERYTHING! I also value honesty, tolerance/acceptance, family, love and kindness to all, especially animals. I believe that if we could all make freedom our highest priority for ourselves and each other, then there would be no war or conflict. Everyone would get to choose, differences would be relished and celebrated, and no one would ever be forced into a way of thinking or being. Our incredibly diverse population would demonstrate the richness and depth of humanity, and we would completely abandon all attempts to get everyone to agree with us and to be the same. When I think of this highest value and describe it to you, I feel empowered and joyful and free. This is my vision for myself and for the world. And I find no conflict among my top five values.

What have you learned about yourself in this process? How does the way you are living your life right now line up with what is truly important to you? What compromises have you made in life that are out of alignment with your values? What changes can you make that will help you to be true to who you really are?

"You are braver than you believe,
stronger than you seem, and smarter
than you think."

- Christopher Robin, (Winnie the Pooh)

CHAPTER 10
INVENTORY YOUR TOOLBOX

You were born with innate abilities, and you've acquired more skills and knowledge along the way. These are talents like singing, dancing, making magic with words through storytelling or writing, figuring out puzzles faster than anyone in your family, being a great listener, being naturally athletic—the list is endless. Take some time to reacquaint yourself with all of the talents you seem to have been born with. Include everything you can think of. Are you really good at math or science, English or art? Were you praised and marveled at because you were good at both math AND English? Remember everything you have ever been good at throughout your life. Awards for spelling bees or prune pit spitting? Voted most likely to succeed? Have you always had a confidence and strength and made your own way, immune to peer pressure? Think of all the ways in which you shine, all the aspects that make you unique. Are you the person that everyone comes to for advice on love, money, business, or health? What are the things that you instinctively *know*?

Now, what have you learned? List every accomplishment, skills you have gained and/or mastered, as well as any degrees, certifications, and courses completed. What are all of the things you already know how to do? What are things you think you have an aptitude for that you're interested in learning? Do you love astrology and remember everything you ever read about it? Do you love getting to the bottom of the story regarding history? Is your home the envy of everyone who sees it because the décor is so beautiful and welcoming? Do you have the yard and garden that everyone wants to copy or hang out in? Are you an expert at needlepoint, cross-stitching, macramé, baking, cooking, or making up recipes? List everything that you know how to do and leave nothing out.

By now you should be getting a glimpse of the enormous and endless possibilities that are right here for you, that equip you to build exactly the life you want! You're more capable than you knew, more talented than you imagined, and already have everything you need to start being in love with your life right this minute!

"Passion is energy. Feel the power that comes from focusing on what excites you."

– Oprah Winfrey

CHAPTER 11
IDENTIFY YOUR PASSIONS

Passion is the fuel that keeps your fire going! When you feel very strongly about something, your energy is magnified, your focus is laser-sharp, and your purpose is so very clear. Are you passionate about helping people get healthy? About animal welfare? Raising happy and healthy children? Racial equality? Caring for the planet? Building community? Think back to your values and the things you discovered throughout this section. Where do your passions lie? Start by listing everything that MIGHT be a passion, then review your list for intensity. Can you narrow it down to just one or two of your greatest loves? You might be like me and have a very long list of things that you are somewhat passionate about, some of which come and go. Or you might be one of those people who has a short list that you are VERY passionate about. You might have a mixture. Don't work at it, have fun with it. Get in touch with what you really care about.

PART III
CREATING A NEW STORY

"If you can imagine it, you can achieve it. If you can dream it, you can become it." ~William Arthur Ward

Congratulations! You've done the work and gained a whole lot of amazing new insight into what you love and who you really are. Now it's time to create the new dream story of your newly discovered path!

"The future belongs to those who believe
in the beauty of their dreams."

- Eleanor Roosevelt

CHAPTER 12
WRITE THE NEW STORY OF YOUR DREAM LIFE

As you've seen in previous chapters, your words, both written and spoken, are extremely powerful in creating your life. Now that you have looked closely at yourself, your life, and reminded yourself of what you really love, it's time to commit your story to paper. This is not the story that was programmed into your head by other people and your own life experiences. Not one that was taught to you in school or church. This is YOUR story, exactly how you want to live it, with people you love, places that nurture your soul, work that fulfills you, and money that powers it all, candy-coated with joy and excitement and satisfaction.

There are several ways of looking at this activity. You could project yourself out into the future, say three to ten years from now, and write the story of how you want your life to look then. Or maybe it doesn't feel good or fun to look that far ahead and you just want to write about your life in one year. Relax. You can't get it wrong and you never get it done. Don't try to force your imagination into a place that it doesn't want to go. If you can't honestly feel like a mansion, millions of dollars, or starring in a blockbuster movie is a possibility for you, don't dream that big.... yet. With practice, you will let life teach you that everything is possible, and even those seemingly unattainable dreams will feel way more natural, like your birthright.

Start where you are. In my story, when I was at my lowest point, my deepest yearning was for freedom, peace, and ease. I couldn't imagine changing careers, but I could imagine finding a new situation within my field that would feel good to me. I could imagine being independent and free to make my own schedule and work the way I wanted to, to have no cap on my income, to have a product to sell that I could believe in and feel good about. I could imagine being able to work from home or anywhere and interacting with people I liked and respected. Even though this had NOT been my most recent experience, I knew without a doubt that it was possible, so that went into my vision.

I identified the heaviest burdens I carried and figured out how to put them down. As mentioned earlier, I had spent my life thinking that I was responsible for the health and wellbeing of various members of my family. So I put into my vision that they were all able to find their own path to happiness and freedom; that I could be there to provide love and assistance WHEN ASKED and where possible; and that I could trust that the Universe would take care of them, just like it was taking care of me.

During my low time, I had treated my body with a lot of disrespect—drinking, smoking, taking diet drugs, and trying to force it into the shape I thought would make it lovable and beautiful. When I started applying these tools to create my new story, I decided to relax, stop bossing my body around and instead find a new way of being with it. I ditched the diet drugs, quit smoking, became more aware and intentional about my alcohol intake, and figuring out other ways to feel good without abusing my body. Being healthy and comfortable in my own skin became a part of my vision.

By that time, I had been without my own home for about four years, so I had a deep longing for a place of my own that felt permanent, safe, and free. I figured out what that looked like and that went into my vision as well. The wellbeing of my beloved cats and dogs was also a major factor when imagining my perfect home. For years, their lives had been restricted and dangerous, and one of my deepest desires was for them to be free, safe, and happy. Thus, a large piece of land for my home, far from other people and cars, became a part of my vision so they could come and go as they pleased.

I was tired of making all the wrong choices in relationships, so I took some time to explore new ways of being. I wanted to bring myself to a place where I could be alone and happy, so that any new relationships would add to and multiply my joy and freedom. Therefore, being in touch with and content with me became a part of my vision.

I have always wanted to be a writer, so that went into my vision as well.

I laid out this vision in 2012, and by 2014 the Universe and I had co-created most of this amazing life. Does this mean I'm done? Absolutely not! My currently reality is just a beautiful launching pad for my next fantastic dream and vision. Your dream story is a living, breathing document that evolves as you learn and grow and discover more about yourself. This feeling of becoming and growing and living into your dreams is exhilarating and fun! You're never postponing your happiness until the arrival of any part of your dream. Your dream adds fun and joy and anticipation and eagerness to your NOW. It's not a longing for something different; it is a joyful faith that life will continue to get better and better.

GUIDELINES FOR AN AMAZING DREAM STORY

When I decided to be a Happiness Coach, I figured out pretty quickly that knowing how to *do* something is quite different from knowing how to *teach* it. The moment I realized I needed help with this, the Universe brought Mary Morrissey to my attention. I studied at the Life Mastery Institute for two years to learn to be a Dream Builder Coach and Life Mastery Consultant. This is where I really learned the value and power of creating a vision. What I had done up until this point was happily accidental, the result of studies from Mike Dooley and Abraham Hicks on visualization and acting "as if." As I learned and grew, I got even better at all aspects of deliberate creation.

Here is what I learned from Mary about creating a vision (summarized and distilled from my own experience). A vision that is worthy of YOU is:

1. Written in the present tense
2. Bathed in gratitude and appreciation
3. Written in the positive
4. Full of emotion and color
5. Open-ended so the Universe has room to improve on your vision

To give you an example, I'll share what my long-ago vision looked like:

I am so happy and grateful now that I have created a life for myself that is secure, safe, serene, and free. I love the work that I do in advertising sales. I love that I am earning the money I need to rebuild my life with endless potential to earn more and more. I am so appreciative that I am free to work on my own schedule and build my business the way I want to. I am grateful that my "employer" is supportive but uninvolved. It feels so good to be paid according to what I produce, feeling free to spend my time exactly as I choose to. I love that I am getting better and better at saving and managing money, secure in the knowledge that everything I need has already been given.

It feels so good to see my treasured family members making their own way in life, figuring things out, and making their lives in their own way. I feel so light and hopeful now that I am trusting that they are okay and feeling only love, appreciation, and acceptance for them.

I LOVE my new home, how it looks and feels and the safe haven it provides for me. It's small and cozy, but feels spacious and natural, with a warm fire and beautiful views. There is a lot of wood and other natural materials and it's surrounded by trees and mountains. The silence and serenity are perfect as it is isolated and far from traffic and other noise. My pets are SO happy! They can come and go as they please through their own door, free to play in the woods, lounge in the sun, or come inside and curl up on the couch.

We LOVE to go for long walks and picnics at lunchtime on a weekday! I love sleeping until my body wants to wake up, having no time schedule to adhere to, indulging myself to work or play, write or create any way and anytime I like.

My body thrives from the fresh air and sunshine and long walks in the woods. I have space and freedom and privacy to explore any kind of physical activity I want to try like yoga or Pilates. Even though I am in the wilderness, I can get to civilization easily anytime I want to shop or have lunch with friends or see new things. I love learning about nutrition and being creative in the kitchen.

I have the best of everything! I love knowing that the Universe will continue sending so much more for my best life. This, or something better still.

As you can see, though this vision was simple and general it was also full of feeling and color and love. If you're like most people, in the beginning you may be asking questions, "Do I deserve this?"; "Am I worthy of this?"; "Is this possible?" Well, as we've been discussing throughout this book, you ARE worthy; you are precious and divine and were meant to live a joyous and full life. All things are possible; if you can dream it, the Universe can deliver it. You just have to learn to use the power of your thoughts and words to call it into being. So begin to ask instead, "Is this a dream worthy of ME? Is it worth dedicating my hours, attention, and energy to? Does this vision measure up to the awesomeness of me and my potential?"

Let's look a little more closely at the five components of a well-crafted life story.

Remember, the first two components are that it is *written in the present tense* and *bathed in gratitude and appreciation.* For example, "I am so happy and grateful now that...!" The intention is to begin living as if all of your dreams have already come true. This is your mission statement for your life so you want to really be able to step into it, live into it, on purpose and mindfully, every day. Be the person who is living this life. What does she wear? Who does she talk to? What kinds of conversations does she have? How does she feel about her life and the world? Be that! Do that!

The third component is that it is *written in the positive.* For example, "I feel so light and hopeful now that I am trusting that they are okay and feeling only love, appreciation and acceptance for them," as opposed to a negative statement such as, "I no longer feel responsible, obligated, or burdened by the problems of my family."

Another example around money might be:

Positive: "I love having healthy bank accounts and zero balances on my credit accounts."

Negative: "I am out of debt."

See how that works?

The fourth component is that your story should be *full of emotion and color.*

Recall when I wrote about my home: "I LOVE my new home, how it looks and feels and the safe haven it provides for me. It's small and cozy, but feels spacious and natural, with the warm fire and beautiful views." When I read this sentence, I FEEL the warmth of the fireplace and the beauty outside. Even when I was sitting in my tiny, dark, basement apartment, I could transport myself in my mind to the new setting I was calling into my reality.

And finally, the fifth component: *your story should be open-ended so the Universe has room to improve on your vision.* The Universe has NO limitations on what it can provide for you. Your deepest, fondest wishes are known and everything is working out for your best good, in perfect timing. When I thought I had found the home that I wanted and things didn't work out, I knew it was because something better awaited me. The home I found was SO much better and half the price. Remember, this or something better still.

The length of your vision is not important. You can keep it simple, or include as many details as you want to bring you joy and clarity. One page or one hundred, this is your new story and you get to write it, add to it, or change it any way you like. This is not a commitment set in stone—it's a dream, a touchstone, a guideline, and map to help guide you towards your happiest life situations—so make it fun, creative, and freeing!

A strong, positive vision will help you in any decision. You simply ask yourself, "Is this in the direction of my dream?" If it's not, you say no. If it is, you say yes. How much easier does that make life, right?

"The cost of a thing is the amount of what I will call life, which is required to be exchanged for it, immediately or in the long run."

- Henry David Thoreau

CHAPTER 13
TEST YOUR NEW STORY. IS IT WORTHY OF YOU?

Creating and living out your new story will require you to spend your resources (time, energy, attention, and devotion) in that direction. Make sure that you have written a new story worthy of all these riches.

Mary Morrissey's test of your vision asks four questions.

1. Does reading my vision make me feel alive and excited?
2. Do I need help from my source (higher power) to create this life?
3. Does my new story require me to grow?
4. Is there good to be created for others and the world?

Now, let's break these down.

Reading and engaging with your new story will become a part of your daily morning ritual. And as you read it, you should feel yourself tingling with joy and anticipation, smiling and loving every minute of imagining how this feels. If it's boring or makes you feel bad in any way, change it! Dig deeper into what you really love and add some elements that make your heart sing. You're going to BE the person living this life starting right this minute, so it should feel amazing!

You are so not alone in this life. The Universe has your back and your best interests covered, and the more you know this in your heart the richer and more fulfilling each moment of your life will be. This is a spiritual journey. Every single atom of this physical world is infused with spirit, especially you. When you focus your intention on getting aligned with your source, your universe expands, your heart grows, and your joy deepens. If you could do it all on your own, without tapping into infinite power and intelligence, you would have done it already, so be sure spiritual growth is a part of your new story.

In my original vision, there was a lot I needed to learn and many ways I needed to grow in order to have the life I wanted. I needed to get better at managing my time and energy and getting work done without supervision or pressure. I needed to get better at managing money. I needed to re-train my brain to look around always for things to appreciate, to learn to pause and consider my responses instead of reacting to "what is." Growth is part of this human experience, and we always need to grow in order to up-level our lives. When creating your new story, ask yourself, "Do I already know everything I need to know to create this new life?" If you do, it's time to make your dream bigger.

Don't be too quick to judge your vision as being "selfish" just because you don't intend to provide clean water for the whole world or end world hunger. If your dream is to grow flowers, you're sharing beauty with the world. If your dream is to find your soulmate, everyone who sees your love will be uplifted by it. Very few dreams or wishes are purely for you with no benefit for others, but be sure. A dream that is worthy of you will create a ripple effect (directly or indirectly) of good that makes a positive impact on the world and expands the Universe.

PART IV
NEW WAYS OF "BEING", LIVING, AND CREATING YOUR NEW LIFE

"It is our choices, Harry, that show what we truly are, far more than our abilities." ~ Professor Dumbledore, *Harry Potter and the Chamber of Secrets*

Now that you have figured out what you want, how you want to feel, and who you want to be, how do we make that happen? This section is full of tools and life skills that will help you learn to manage your own perspective, choose your responses, and be the master of your mood. Happiness and freedom are a choice! Learn how to choose.

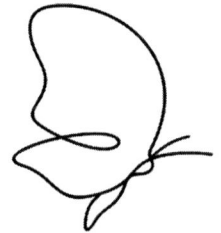

"Morning is an important time of day, because how you spend your morning can often tell you what kind of day you are going to have."

– Lemony Snicket

CHAPTER 14
MAGNIFICENT MANIFESTING MORNINGS

The thoughts you think start a chain reaction that changes everything in your world, so it stands to reason that the first few moments of your day are bright, shining opportunities to choose thoughts that feel incredible. A positive, uplifting thought attracts other, like thoughts that evoke positive feelings; these in turn spark inspired beautiful action that produces amazing manifestations. Even if you do nothing except feel great, this wave of positive vibration spreads from you like ripples in a pond, transforming everything it its path and attracting the resources, people, and ideas you need to be in love with your life. This is the true magic of life, the law of attraction. In the words of Wayne Dyer, "Change your thoughts, change your life."

BEGIN YOUR DAY ON PURPOSE BEFORE YOU EVEN OPEN YOUR EYES

Hopefully you have the luxury of sleeping until your body and soul have completed their nightly journey of rest and exploration and your mornings can start when and how you want them to. If this is not the case—if you wake up to an alarm clock, not feeling rested or excited about your day—consider some changes that you can make right now. Would you LOVE to be able to sleep until you wake naturally? Put that in your vision! In the meantime, if you are on a schedule that requires you to wake at a certain time in the morning, back up a step and get yourself in bed as early as you need to for a full night of sleep. Most people do best with seven to nine hours of sleep, but our society has a tendency to make sleep seem like a waste of time, something indulged in by lazy people. Let that go, and give yourself permission to get the rest your mind, body, and soul want! Brag about how MUCH sleep you get, instead of how little. More on your relationship with sleep in the upcoming chapters.

While you're sleeping, all the momentum created by your thoughts and experiences stops. Your slate is wiped clean and you get to start the next day fresh! The problem is that most of us learn to just pick up our problems and worries right where we left them the night before. You don't have to do this. You can make a new choice to start fresh and on purpose, as the master of your attitude and your day.

Before you even open your eyes, decide that you are going to have a bright shiny day full of appreciation. What can you think of right now that makes you smile, that shines a light on the lovely aspects of your life? Are you lying beside the love of your life? Is your bed comfy, warm, and luxurious? Do you have the best pillow EVER? Are there things in your day or week that you are really looking forward to? Did something amazing happen yesterday that you can replay in your mind and evoke those great feelings again? I currently have two orange kitties that sleep on my bed most every night, and I know that as soon as I turn on the light they are going to sit up and blink sleepily and adorably at me. That thought alone makes me smile. I think of them, I feel so empowered in knowing that I can get up right then, or sleep a little more, or read...I feel such appreciation that I get to live my life in every moment exactly as I choose. I have a long list of "go-to" aspects that I can bring to mind first thing to start off my days on purpose, happy, and free.

Create your own list and gather tools to help you with this first, oh-so-important moment of your day. If you use an alarm, make it play your favorite song. Put a picture of a treasured person or memory beside your bed. Make a list of things that make you smile and bring it to mind or actually read it as soon as you open your eyes. Is there a perfume or fragrance that stirs your soul and brings back memories that you love? Put that beside your bed and have a whiff. Do you look forward to that cup of coffee each morning? Set your coffeemaker to brew automatically so that lovely, robust aroma is the first thing you smell. Is your bed fresh and clean and nice-smelling so you can deliberately notice and appreciate that? The very act of gathering these tools and setting these intentions is putting things in motion for you to start your day off in a happy mood. In time, this will reset your subconscious and your default wake-up state will be one of joy and appreciation.

Once you've purposely created this great mood, make a conscious decision to maintain this feeling as long as possible. When you first start, you might not even make it to the bathroom before something goes "wrong" or you remember something that displeases you. With practice, you can learn to keep this great feeling for longer and longer until you find yourself feeling awesome all day! I promise, once you get used to feeling this high-flying and happy, you will be very particular about what you allow to affect you.

Let's say, for example, that you feel your mood plummet

when you turn on the news. Now you have a decision to make. Tomorrow, will you care more about the skewed information others are dishing out, or about how you're feeling and the kind of day you're creating? You're a grownup. You get to decide. Maybe you feel great until you check your email and find "problems" to solve that tank your mood. You might postpone opening your email until later in the morning, giving yourself more time to cement your deliberate good feeling place. Teach yourself how to stay in that place for as long as possible.

Now, make your bed! This is sending a clear signal to your subconscious and to the Universe that you are putting away the things you're finished with, and looking forward to getting into a tidy space with smooth bedding at the end of the day. Your space is sacred. Your sleep is sacred. Honor yourself, your home, and your body by treating your bed with reverence and care. I like to put a big piece of selenite on my bed to clear the energy and prepare a pure place for my next night's sleep. Create your own sense of ceremony and ritual around your waking time.

CREATE A MORNING SPIRITUAL RITUAL

> *"We are not human beings having a spiritual experience. We are spiritual beings having a human experience."* ~ *Pierre Teilhard de Chardin*

Understanding the above quote is foundational, and the most important and powerful part of the process of learning to be happy and free. It could be called your relationship with spirit; however, since you *are* spirit, it could just as appropriately be called your relationship with YOU. There is no separation between the Source that created you and yourself, so you need not "seek" a connection with your source; it is always there. It is breathing you and beating your heart and flowing to and through you always. Your spiritual practice is designed to help you know, feel, and flow with the great power that is you and live every moment of your life from this place of faith and joy. I am not for or against any religion, doctrine, or spiritual practice—your connection with God, Source, your Highest Self, the Universe, or whatever you choose to call it, is highly personal and intimate. My youth was filled with many hours of bible study and the doctrine taught by the Southern Baptists; today, I love to study Buddhism, Hinduism, Wicca, The Tao, Chinese I Ching, Astrology, ancient mythology, magick, and anything else that crosses my path and piques my interest. I love Human Design, which combines many ancient and modern methods and is based on your birthdate, time, and place.

My morning spiritual ritual has elements of lots of different studies and is always evolving as I discover new ways of feeling my connection to my source. I love the wonder and magic of the elements—air, water, fire, and earth. I love the miracle of nature, the cycles of seasons, and the moon. All of these elements make their way in and out of my sacred spiritual time as they speak to me. Your morning spiritual ritual is YOUR way of spending time relishing and nourishing your connection, filling yourself up with the awesome knowledge of the power that is you. I am a true lover of ritual! It fills any activity—even mundane things like doing the dishes or washing your hair—with reverence and fun and importance. It teaches you to BE the spiritual being that you are.

A morning ritual that is sacred to you, honored, revered, and adhered to will help put you firmly in the driver's seat of your life. There are many things you can do in the morning to establish a morning ritual that will help you to live your life in happiness and freedom. Try them out, see what feels good to you, and have fun! See yourself as the powerful, wise, godlike being that is literally casting magic spells and creating your day. Here are some suggestions to get you started:

First, gather some tools that feel good and speak to your intention, such as symbols from your faith, candles, crystals, incense, essential oils, or music. Then, create a space specifically for your morning ritual and treat it with reverence. I have a corner of my loft bedroom that is dedicated to all that I consider sacred; in fact, I'm writing this in my sacred space now! You might also set a time for this ritual, if this appeals to you, and put it on your calendar. Your journal is vital to your morning ritual, of course, but what other items can you add to your sacred space to create a feeling of reverence, help you focus, and add power to this time?

JOURNALING

Most of us spend more time planning a two-week vacation than we do planning our lives. Make your journal your life-planning tool! I have a journal/planner that I write in every single day. It's my life companion, a place where I make friends with my thoughts, interact with my desires, set my intentions, and choose where I put my focus. I record everything here, from appointments and shopping/wish lists to plans and dreams and schemes. I also keep track of the lunar cycle and sometimes my food and movement. Sometimes I have separate books for journaling, scheduling, and other writing practices, and I always have one or more cherished blank books to create in. No matter what, there are a few things that go into my journal every day. The first is My Magic Orchid. It's based on a cherished story my mom told me when I was a little girl.

The Magic Orchid

There was once a woman who lived in a very cluttered and untidy home. We don't really know the reason—maybe she just never learned to keep a nice home, or maybe she knew how but didn't have the energy to keep up her house because she was depressed, or heartbroken, or both. At any rate, she was miserable and her surroundings were a direct reflection of her internal state.

One day, a delivery person brought to her door a lovely orchid plant. It had no card and the messenger did not say from whence it came, so the woman accepted the gift, perplexed but feeling a small spark of pleasure ignite in her heart. This plant was extraordinary, with a breathtakingly beautiful flower, and the woman took great pleasure in just looking at it.

After a time she decided to put the plant down, but when she looked around her messy home she could not find a spot for it. She placed the plant gently on the floor at her feet, chose a crowded table in her sitting room, and got to work. When she had cleared a space, she reverently placed the plant in the clear space and stood back to admire it again. At first, she just basked in the beauty of the plant and marveled at how its warmth seemed to spread out into the room. Then she noticed the clutter that was still on the rest of the table and thought how much prettier the plant would be when the table was completely clear.

When she finished cleaning the table, she noticed that the beautiful plant and table were very out of place in the untidy room, so she set about straightening, organizing, dusting, and cleaning the room. At some point she heard someone humming happily and was startled to realize it was her! She kept on cleaning until the entire room was bright and sparkling, a worthy setting for the beautiful plant. By now she was feeling exhilarated, but also a little tired and thirsty, so she decided to take the plant into the kitchen with her while she made a snack and a cup of tea.

Instantly she noticed that her kitchen did not match her pretty sitting room and there was no place to put her plant. The process repeated itself, and before she knew it she had a sparkling kitchen and was beginning to feel herself full of hope and accomplishment. Her efforts then spread to her entire house, to her yard, to her person, and to her life. Before too long, this woman was thinking in a clear way, living in a clear way, and thriving in the uncluttered space in her home and in her mind. The Magic Orchid lived on and was often moved from room to room with the woman as her appreciation for the plant, and her life, continued to expand and fill with more and more joy.

There are so many ways to learn from this sweet story. So many messages and interpretations.

One is that no matter the depths of your despair, you can take one small step, then another and so on, in the direction of joy. Those steps get easier and easier, longer and longer, until you are striding confidently in the direction of the life you want.

Another lesson is to do what we can, with what we have, from where we are. When the woman looked at her whole house and the mess that permeated every corner, it seemed impossible to fix. Similarly, cleaning up an entire life is a daunting task, but clearing one small space from which to start is very possible. Baby steps will take you to the top of the highest mountain, as long as you keep taking them.

Chapter 14 - Magnificent Manifesting Mornings

At the end of your life, you will not regret the things you did, no matter how they turn out. But you will regret the things you didn't do, the risks you didn't take, or the adventures and joys that you missed out on because of fear or doubt. Your potential is literally unlimited, but you must make the choice to begin to live into that potential, to expand your capacity and really start to grow into the next best version of yourself. Today is the BEST time to start taking responsibility for your life, to realize that you are a creator and begin to create *deliberately*.

Each day, choose one Magic Orchid for the day. This is any thought that always makes you smile. It could be the face of a child, a memory of a perfect day, a person, pet, or dream—any thought that you can always return to if you find your day or mood going off course. Your Magic Orchid will almost instantly raise your vibration and your point of attraction. It's a touchstone that you can return to at any point in your day when you want to feel better.

Just the act of choosing your Magic Orchid is, well, magic! If you're in a place that feels sad and lonely, consciously sifting through everything you know to find something lovely to think about will train your brain to look for the positive. No matter how things are going, you can find one thing to appreciate that will help you to turn things to an upward spiral. On the flipside, if things are going great and you are feeling on top of the world, sifting through all that wonderfulness to choose just one will amplify your feelings of abundance and love and appreciation. After a while, you might begin choosing the same things again, but try your best in the first thirty days to choose a new Magic Orchid each day.

AFFIRMATIONS AND I AM STATEMENTS

Remember how we made the decision to live as if our dream life was already here? This is where we step very specifically into that intention and begin to declare to the Universe that we have arrived!

There is nothing more powerful than "I AM" statements, so always follow those words with something wonderful. Also, play with the wording so it feels believable and uplifting to you. There are many great sources of affirmations and these can be fantastic inspiration *if* you happen to be in alignment with the message already. If not, it could have the opposite effect. For instance, if you're worried about how to make rent and you read a card that says, "I am a money magnet and always have more than enough," it might just piss you off and make you feel even worse.

Some of my favorite I AM statements are, "I am strong, healthy, and vibrant"; "I am prosperous"; "I am in love with my life"; "I am creative and focused"; "I am patient and kind"; "I AM the deliberate and joyous creator of my life!" What statements most resonate with you?

I AM CREATING/INVITING/WELCOMING/PREPARING FOR STATEMENTS

More than likely, you have a giant to-do list that seems to keep growing each day. You're always thinking about all of the things that are left undone, instead of giving yourself credit for what you DID do. Most of us are in a mindset of making things happen, pushing and striving, and trying. Your I Am Creating statements are a softer way of setting intentions, deciding what you want to welcome into your life, what you want to create, and how you want your life to go. These statements set you up for success and establish you as a co-creator with the source that created all. While organizing your thoughts and intentions into lists can be fun and focusing and helpful, it can also be daunting and overwhelming. This is why I suggest choosing just three things that you want to manifest in your life and painting a broad picture of "how" they get done. This creates a free-feeling, bright, and optimistic place from which to take action in your life.

Each morning, choose your three things that you would like to accomplish or see progress on. This book, for instance, has been on my Creation list every day for a while and will be until it's finished. In doing so, I set myself up to be inspired and enthusiastic, to be guided by Source, and connected to Infinite Intelligence. I imagine my brain and spirit having access to all that is, ever was, and ever will be, and prepare to be enlightened. This is also a very good time to think about your "why." Why do you care about what you are creating? My "why" is that I want to help. I want to share what I have learned and give you the tools to live your best life ever, in every moment. Of course I have other projects that come and go all the time, so I set my intention for the best outcomes of those as well, but again, no more than three! This is a place to decide who you want to be and what the broad strokes of your life look like. By all means, break things down into specific tasks and pieces on another list if you like. But here, set your big intentions.

If you are seeking financial peace and freedom, your statements might be "I am creating financial peace and freedom" or "I am welcoming resources and ideas for financial health." I included this type of creation statement for a while and received a windfall that allowed me to wipe out almost all of my interest-bearing debt. What a feeling!

Dream big here and teach yourself to have big expectations. Then live your day as if they have already come to pass. BE the person who is living this life already. Happy and free on purpose.

DREAM STORY INTERACTION

Remember the dream story you wrote in Chapter 8? Well, now it's time for you to read and engage with that story, to remind yourself to BE the person who is living that dream. Do you have a magnificent home and vast gardens? A working farm? Are you a best-selling author or songwriter? Running your own local or international business? Traveling around the world? Growing vegetables or flowers? Waking up every morning beside the love of your life? Whatever is in your vision for your dream life, get in touch with that and write a few keywords to remind you and connect you with this higher purpose. These can be general words like health, wealth, freedom, fame, love, and community and/or specific words like "thriving local art store"; "popular yoga studio"; or "six amazing trips per year." Now, BE that person! What does she wear? How does she feel? How does she spend her time? Who does she hang out with? What physical things can you do right now to begin creating that feeling? Be the person living the life of your dreams and prepare to be amazed at how your life evolves!

MEDITATION

"I have lived with several Zen masters—all of them cats."
~ Eckhart Tolle

I firmly believe that every conscious being benefits from a regular meditation practice. It brings about spiritual awakening, lowers blood pressure, creates better responses to stress and other stimuli, and a host of other things too numerous to list in this book. There are also thousands of ways to meditate, and you can't get it "wrong." You just need to just sit quietly, deliberately, and on purpose for a specified amount of time. I studied with spiritual teacher and stress management expert davidji for my Masters of Wisdom and Meditation certification, but I continue to study from other masters, seeing different viewpoints and trying different things. Your meditation practice will continue to grow and change as you do, so just get started and enjoy yourself.

If you have never meditated before start with just five to ten minutes. If you're a "crisis" meditator or have a hit-or-miss meditation practice, decide to be more reverent and deliberate about a daily practice. Do meditate around the same time every day. Make your practice important enough to have its own time slot in your schedule. Mine is sometime between when I wake up and eight a.m., when my day officially begins with caring for my pets. Somedays I meditate for an hour, other days for only ten minutes, but I make sure to do it every morning.

Be comfortable! If you are sitting in a place that feels safe and calm, in a position and on a surface that feels good to your body, you are much more likely to come back day after day. Comfort is queen!

Add touches to your space and to your meditation that make it feel sacred and special. I suggest using candles, incense, crystals, and other items sacred to you or your faith. Give yourself a facial or foot massage right before or after to add an even greater feeling of self-care to your meditation ritual.

PART V
SPECIFIC FOCUS ON GENERAL AREAS OF YOUR LIFE

"Whenever you want to achieve something, keep your eyes open, concentrate and make sure you know exactly what it is you want. No one can hit their target with their eyes closed." ~ Paulo Coelho

Money, relationships, and health are the most common areas with which we humans have trouble. For some people, physical fitness is the biggest concern, for others it is their finances or love life. The good news is that when you improve one area of your life, the other areas improve too! All the work you do to build a joyous relationship with your body and your money will spill over into your personal relationships, and so on. This section will help you gain clarity regarding your money, health, and relationships, and show you how to be in love with your home and your daily life. Remember to create each area in joy!

"Take care of your body. It's the only place you have to live."

– Jim Rohn

CHAPTER 15

BE IN LOVE WITH YOUR BODY

Time now to get more specific about managing your perspective in each area of your life. Your body is a good place to begin because you take it everywhere with you. In the earlier chapters, you had a look at how your body is and how you would love it to be. Now let's explore ways to move in the direction of your dream body.

Stop criticizing! Start appreciating.

Begin by making a list of at least twenty-one ways in which your body is currently serving you. Give yourself time and grace to reach twenty-one, then add more if and when you think of them. Here is an example of what your list might look like:

1. My skin is supple and lovely.
2. My heart beats perfectly with no help from me.
3. My lungs perform perfectly with no help from me.
4. My joints are strong and operate smoothly.
5. My hair is shiny.
6. My eyes show me beauty.
7. My belly processes food and sends me the right signals of hunger and satiety.
8. My fingernails grow.
9. My ears translate music and the sweet voices of people I love.

10. My back is strong.
11. My muscles serve me perfectly, supporting me in all that I do.
12. My bones hold my body upright.
13. My immune system protects me.
14. My blood flows freely to all cells in my body, bringing oxygen and life.
15. My brain is clear and clever.
16. My body is agile and flexible.
17. My legs help me run like the wind.
18. My fingers write and type and do amazing things on command.
19. My feet support me and connect me with the sacred earth.
20. My sex organs give me pleasure and the ability to create new life.
21. My arms are great at giving hugs.

Your body is unique, just like you are. Society, however, teaches us that one size and shape is better than another and consistently bombards us with images of those "ideals." We learn that we are not lovable because we are too short or tall; too fat or skinny; our breasts and buttocks are not the right size or shape; our eyes are too small or large, our lashes too short...The list of ways in which women criticize and condemn themselves is endless. Let's learn a new way. Instead of looking in the mirror and picking yourself apart, learn to love yourself, exactly as you are. Understand and embrace the beauty and perfection that is you. This takes practice. Here are some things to try that will help you form new habits of appreciation and banish the habits of self-judgement.

Create reminders, such as mirror notes, that will help you

remember to love and praise yourself. (Louise Hay has wonderful teachings on mirror work.) Use a lipstick or liner and write sweet messages to yourself on your mirrors; or use post-it notes or other paper. Write messages like "Hello Beautiful!" or "I love you, (your name) just like you are"; "Look for beauty!"; "You are AMAZING!"; "You are unique and adored." Use your imagination and experiment with different words and phrases that help you to fall in love with your physical self.

I currently have this quote from Wayne Dyer's *Change Your Thoughts, Change Your Life* in a frame by my backdoor and hanging in my shower:

> *"I Came From GREATNESS! I must be like what I came from. I will never abandon my belief in my greatness and the greatness of others."*

Change these notes often to keep them in your attention. You'll find that after a few days, you forget to notice them; they just become a part of the landscape. Being deliberate and intentional by changing them out will help you to keep your goal in mind. Your goal is to love yourself, exactly as you are!

We also explored the parts of your physical experience that might not be ideal. You may have an illness or diagnosis, feel burdened by extra weight, or have other conditions that are not a part of your dream for yourself. Am I asking you to ignore your condition and symptoms? Sort of. When you are focused on health and vibrancy, illness and dis-ease don't get the attention they need to grow and should atrophy from neglect. If you are treating a disease, like cancer or heart disease, diabetes, or high blood pressure, by all means follow your course of treatment. Do what needs to be done, but then turn your attention back to joy.

When you begin to be really in touch with yourself, with your body, and your higher power, you will be led to the right doctors, medicines, lifestyle, and other choices. Try to relax into this and learn to go with the flow, trusting your own instincts and intuition. Try to ease your mind into an attitude of knowing that everything is working out for the best for you, that you can't get it wrong and you'll never get it done. That health and vibrancy are your birthright and perfectly natural, and that disease and discomfort are "unnatural."

Start a conversation with your body. If you are experiencing pain or discomfort or other unwanted physical symptoms, find out what your body is trying to say. At Life Mastery School, we learned to actually write this dialogue, as if we were scripting a play. For example, you might be suffering from heartburn. Your dialogue might look like this.

> You: Hello body! I've noticed that there is pain from heartburn at night. Is there something you want to tell me?
>
> Body: Hello! Thanks so much for asking. I'm having trouble digesting food while lying down. It might be easier for me if you had dinner earlier so that I'm done with the digesting by the time you go to bed.
>
> You: Thank you! I will be happy to try that. Anything else you want me to know?
>
> Body: Yes. I love you and I wish you wouldn't worry so much. Everything is always working out.

And so on. Your natural state is to feel good. Your body loves you and is doing the very best it can to serve you, using the resources you provide it—food, movement, sleep, and most especially energy. The best thing you can do for your body and your health is to think lovely thoughts and feel beautiful feelings. There's a good reason that "stress" is such a bad word.

The main point is to not let the negative experiences be the star of your show. Instead of talking and thinking constantly about your negative condition, turn your attention to everything that is going well, as in the list you created. Set your sites beyond the condition and make plans for your future. Relishing the thought of travel, parties, and visits with friends and loved ones keeps your vibration high and then all parts of your life MUST meet that high vibration. This is the law. Get to loving your life and focusing on the wanted and let the unwanted heal and disappear from your lack of attention to it.

Now time for some inspired action, in this case making another list to move your body in the direction of vibrant health, and further identify yourself as the creator of your life. You see, even as you are making peace with where you are and being in love with your body just as it is, the woman in your vision is desiring a higher level of health or fitness. For example, I want very much to explore out of the way places, like the outer reaches of Ireland, Scotland, and Norway. I want to see where the Vikings lived and walk the fields of Ireland and hike the jungles of Costa Rica. This means the woman in my vision is very strong and flexible and has great stamina. She has strong legs and is light and agile enough to climb in and out of boats, hike up tall trails, and maneuver around waterfalls. She wants to be able to converse easily in Spanish and maybe even other languages. She wants to feel so in touch with her body that doing yoga or Qigong in San Juan La Laguna, Guatemala feels safe and fun. She has confidence in her body and so is unafraid to try anything.

I do not love "exercise." I would rather do anything than be on a treadmill or stationary bike and I refuse to spend even one minute doing something I don't want to do or that doesn't bring me happiness or peace. My challenge and yours is to find ways to serve our bodies that will help them to have the resilience and strength needed to live our dreams. At the time of this writing, I am carrying some extra fat that might make me feel encumbered on my travels. I've been rather sedentary so I feel like I would benefit from enhancing the strength and flexibility of my muscles, making sure that I feel secure and balanced and sure on my feet and being a little lighter. Here's where the list comes in.

Make a list of twenty-one things you could do or try that might help your body feel the way you want it to and to serve you in the life of your dreams. It might be things you have done in the past (for example, from the list of things you used to love), or new things to explore and try, research and investigate, learn and experience. It is absolutely vital that you move your body in ways that feel good to your whole person—mind, body, and soul. This list will help you to find what that means for you. My list might look like this.

1. Pay attention to the signals my body gives me about food. (What and how much to eat)
2. Try Qigong
3. Try different yoga practices
4. Dance while doing the dishes
5. Do squats while brushing my teeth
6. Hike on my own mountain more often with my dogs
7. Take the dogs to new places to walk and hike and ex-

plore
8. Pretend my mountain is a volcano in Guatemala
9. Work in different positions (standing, sitting on the floor, etc.)
10. Meditate on what my body really wants and needs and be very much in touch with it
11. Park far away from storefronts
12. Look for a place to swim and play in the water
13. Hula hoop while watching fun shows on Netflix
14. Minimize my wine intake
15. Set a reminder to move around every hour
16. Find ways to lift heavy things that are fun and useful
17. Put frequently used things in lower cabinets; squat while removing them
18. Reach and stretch toward the sun and sky and moon every day
19. Do self-massage to deepen the connection with my body
20. Practice amazing self-care by pampering skin and feeling loved and beautiful
21. Examine the effects of caffeine and adjust for great sleep.

Now, look at your dream life. What does the woman in that vision feel like in her body? What ways can you joyfully co-create your own vibrant health and vitality? Decide that you will have an open mind and heart and discover what feels good to you.

Nothing is more important than being fully present, and the happiest version of yourself, in every moment. This is where your power is. You cannot create in the past as it's already gone, and the future has not yet arrived. Never "wait" until you have achieved any goal in order to be happy, because you'll never get there. If you're waiting to be happy until you achieve the ideal body weight or level of fitness, you'll just set a new goal when you get there. Future plans are amazing IF you use them as an excuse to find joy and fun and clarity right now. Think of how this requires you to really manage your perspective. You could have a vacation planned for two months from now and count the days until you can take a break from your life; OR you could decide to enjoy every minute of your daily life and use the excitement and planning of the vacation to uplevel your joy. Never postpone happiness. Never postpone freedom. Be Happy and Free On Purpose in every moment.

NEVER let your physical body dictate your level of happiness. This is the magic of loving yourself just as you are. Even if you are currently experiencing a level of disease that brings you pain, there is a difference between having pain and despair, and having pain and hope. Try your best to relax and allow your pain to heal, putting your attention on the anticipated feelings of relief and healing. Say thank you to your body for your symptoms and take them as signs that your body and your spirit are on the job, healing and repairing and restoring you to your natural state of health. Have conversations with your body. "What do you need? How can I serve you? What messages are you trying to send me?" Make an open line of communication with your precious body a priority.

YOUR RELATIONSHIP WITH FOOD

How you think and feel about food is intimately connected with your relationship with your body and SO much a part of everyday life. And there are so many conflicting messages about what foods and regimens are "good" and "bad"—low-carb, low-fat, organic, non-GMO, trans-fats, vegan, paleo, carnivore, primal, vegetarian, smoothies and juices, fasts and "re-loads." I am a certified Primal Health Coach and still can get mired down in all of the plans and quick fixes and efforting that is presented to us by the fitness industry. The truth is, your body is unique and there is no "perfect plan" that fits everyone. I love the Primal lifestyle as it is a very broad and generous, varied, and an easy place to start. See the links to Mark Sisson, the Primal Blueprint, and others in the Resources section at the end of the book.

You can't just quit eating. Food is necessary for life and, like everything, it's meant to be joyful. You are WAY better off having pizza and beer with hearty enjoyment and pleasure than choking down dry chicken breast and steamed broccoli with misery and resentment. Freedom means you eat what you love and your body thrives. There are no bad or good foods, just foods that you enjoy and work well with your body and those that don't. Please note that when I say food, I do not mean the science experiments that are contained in most pre-packaged meals or snacks. I mean meat, cheese, fish, fowl, vegetables, fruits, even some wild grains—things that are provided by a generous and loving Mother Earth. Get in touch with your own body and your own values and eat what you and your body love and thrive on.

This is by no means a comprehensive guide to food, just the thoughts I'm most passionate about and that I think will serve you the most. First of all, try your best to forget all of the "rules" you have learned throughout a lifetime of diets and quick weight loss plans. Forget about phrases like "no pain no gain" and "crushing it." Begin to believe that health and vitality are natural states that you can return to, not ideals that you must strive for. This means allowing vibrant good health and feeling great; treating your body with honor, love, and respect; and LISTENING to the messages that your body has to share with you regarding, not just food, but everything. Your body is unique and it has unique responses to food. Let it be the boss of what is good for you, not some outside influence. Try different foods and pay attention to how each makes you feel.

Example: There is a giant "gluten-free" movement going on right now that I think is very important to our health as a nation and as a species. I believe everyone has some level of negative response to gluten, as well as all grains and legumes, ranging from celiac (dangerously sensitive to gluten) to something so insignificant they don't even notice it. Personally, I don't feel as amazing as I like to after having grains, so I avoid them in my everyday life. At home, I cook one hundred percent of my meals and use very few pre-packaged items. This really saves on reading labels as mother nature always delivers the perfect product. But when I travel or dine out with friends, I absolutely have the famous pizza from my hometown, tortilla chips at our favorite Mexican restaurant, or the pastry the restaurant specializes in. The joy and fun of those experiences completely offsets any minor negative consequences of having grains. Do I also have the refried beans? No, because my enjoyment of those is not equal to the tummy rumblings that result from legumes.

The antinutrients in grains and legumes cause an immune response in your body. If this is an occasional attack, no big deal; if on the other hand your immune system is always on high alert trying to protect you from damage to your gut from industrialized grains, it gets exhausted and confused, begins striking out everywhere, and then here comes the autoimmune disease. If you are suffering from any of the multiple autoimmune diseases that are so prevalent today, I encourage you to try eliminating grains, healing your gut, and start making discerning, informed food decisions that feel best to you. This is how you have freedom in your relationship with food. You are meant to feel amazing in your body, from birth to death, so use food to nourish and support it in the way that feels good to you.

Another example: almost everyone would agree that beets and turnips are "healthy" but they give me gas and a crampy tummy. There's truth to the phrase "One man's meat is another man's poison." Decide for yourself what foods are beneficial for you and your precious body.

To get really clear on your relationship with food, try keeping a food journal for a week. Write down how you feel before, during, and after you eat. Write down what you ate and why you chose it. See if any patterns emerge. Notice if you are feeling guilty or self-critical about any of your choices. Notice if your body responds in specific ways to specific foods.

Of course, ritual will serve you here as well. Take a moment before you start eating to bring yourself fully into the present, to feel appreciation for your meal, to connect with your body, and set your intention to get great pleasure and nourishment from what you're eating. Take the time to notice how your body is responding. Create at least one ritual per month that is centered around food. If you can have a regular family meal time, that's wonderful. Or maybe you have lunch or dinner with friends once a month, or a potluck party. Many traditions revolve around food. Create your own; notice and enjoy the ones you already have.

RELATIONSHIP WITH SLEEP

Food and sleep are the first priorities to nourish a healthy body, yet many have developed a disdain for sleep, especially in the US. Sleep is precious! It is a time when all momentum stops, your slate is wiped clean, and you get to start fresh. As mentioned earlier, seven to nine hours a night is best for most people, but again, your body is unique, so structure your life in the way that feels best to you and allows your body to rest when and how long it wants to. Many successful people, "go-getters," like to brag about how little sleep they need and imply that sleeping is a waste of time. Trust me, you can be just as successful, have more fun, and enjoy life more if you honor your body and get good sleep. If you love to nap, do it! If you wake in the middle of the night, don't stress, just be okay with being awake and go back to sleep when it feels good to you. There's no right or wrong way to sleep, despite many traditions that say otherwise. I feel best when I go to sleep before ten and wake up somewhere between four and six a.m. I tend to sleep more in the winter when nights are long, and less in the summer. Honor your own unique rhythms and desires and be okay when they ebb and flow. When you have a project that you are really engaged in and excited about, you may feel more energetic and feel good on less sleep; during those in-between times when things are slower, you may want to loll about and sleep ten hours. Do what feels good! Love your body as it loves you.

RELATIONSHIP WITH MOVEMENT (EXERCISE)

Finally, the fitness industry has taught us that chronic cardio is good for us and that we should be spending hours on the treadmill or bicycle. Refer to the story of Mark Sisson for more about how this lifestyle can ruin your body. He is my fitness mentor and founder of Primal Health Institute where I got my Primal Health Coach Certification. Your body wants to move in a way that is totally unique to you! You may be someone who is full of energy and needs to have daily exercise in order to spend the excess and get good sleep. You may be a lower-energy person who really doesn't have this need. Pay attention to what you love and the signals your body gives you. Do activities that you love. Try a lot of things and see what speaks to your soul and feels good to your body. You might be a person who LOVES to run! Running might feel like total freedom to you and your body may relish it. You might love the grace and connection of yoga or Qigong. You might love to dance or hula-hoop, go swimming, hiking, or on long walks, or doing yardwork—the ways in which you can move your body are endless, so find what feels good to you and your body and enjoy! If you are forcing yourself through some horrid workout that you dread and despise, your results will be short-lived at best and harmful at worst. Life is supposed to be fun! We'll have an entire section coming up on teaching you to "Never Do Anything That You Don't Want to Do."

Make a list of ways to move your body that MIGHT feel good to you. This isn't a commitment or a to-do list. It's simply a way of activating your interest and intention and becoming open to new ways of moving. When you write "take some long walks" on your list, you might get a call from a friend inviting you to take a stroll in the park. When you get open to ideas, more will come and the perfect ways of moving your body will be revealed to you.

YOUR RELATIONSHIP WITH YOUR BREATH

Have you ever found yourself so stressed out that you actually forget to breathe? Or maybe you breathe shallowly, in a way that doesn't fully nourish your body. It is easy to ignore your breathing because it is automatic, reliable, and requires no effort on your part. However, it is also a miracle and the ever-present proof of the energy that beats your heart. Concentrating on your breath in meditation; learning to be conscious of it and to breathe through your nose and not your mouth; and taking the time to connect with your breath throughout your day all are great ways of honoring this miracle. Breath is life. Relish it, be aware of and grateful for it. There is a Breathe app on the Apple watch that I find really awesome. It reminds you to pause and just breathe for an amount of time that you decide. Just one minute of paying attention and being deliberate about your breath calms your mind and your nervous system. Breathe on purpose. Breathe into all the parts of your body. Deliberately think of nourishing each of your cells with life-giving oxygen and elements of air.

Believe it or not, there are ways to breathe that are more beneficial for you. For instance, there are breathing coaches like Oxygen Advantage that teach you to always breath through your nose, at a certain speed. If you want to delve deeper into that, head to for www.behappyfirst.org/57 for a great interview with my fellow meditation teacher Chantal Pitkamaki on The How to Choose Happiness and Freedom Show. There are also links from there to learn more about Oxygen Advantage. You can also check out the complete science and study on the best ways to breathe in the Resources section.

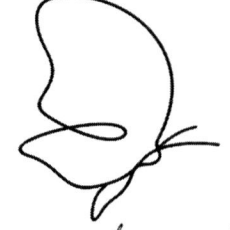

"If you judge people, you have no time to love them."

– Mother Teresa

CHAPTER 16

FALL BACK IN LOVE WITH LOVE AND YOUR LOVED ONES

Human beings are social creatures. In primitive times, being liked and cooperative was actually a survival requirement, as dissenters could be expelled from the community and unlikely to make it alone on a dangerous planet.

Relationships are also one of those areas in which we are really prone to giving away our power. Examine your beliefs and vocabulary around your primary relationships. Do you believe that you can only be happy if they are happy? Do you use some version of the phrase "makes me," as in "He makes me so mad!" or "You're making me crazy"? Reframe your thoughts and beliefs and implant the understanding that no one can make you feel or do anything, or keep you from doing anything. "He won't let me" is another common disempowering belief and phrase. You don't have to wait for outside circumstances, like the behavior of other people, to change in order for you to be happy. Imagine the power of choosing to feel good, no matter what, compared to insisting that everyone and everything line up just perfectly (which is never going to happen). If you think you don't have time for self-care because of the demands of your family, change that belief. You will be such a joy to your family and the world when you take time to take care of you! As women, we have an innate desire to serve and nurture and this is wonderful and amazing. But you can't serve from an empty vessel, so remember to fill yourself up first! Your joy and happiness will shine light on everyone who sees you. Your children will be inspired by your pleasant and positive outlook and everyone will want to be around you, basking in the warmth of your love.

No one else needs to change even one thing for you to be happy. Remember the "find the squares" exercise from Chapter 5? You see what you're looking for. If you're looking for fault in the behavior of your loved ones, you are certain to find it. If you're looking for lovable qualities, you're certain to find those instead! When you notice, praise, and express appreciation for the wonderful things they do, they will want to do more of those things. When you pressure them to behave in a certain way or try to exert control, they will rebel and continue to show you more of what you're criticizing. This is the case with every single person. We would all love to be better people, but we also want to have the power to make our own choices. When your husband or child behaves the way you want them to in order to avoid your rage or otherwise keep the peace, you are robbing them of the joy of making their own choices. Empower yourself! Empower your loved ones! Practice unconditional love and watch that come back to you tenfold.

Some relationships are just not ideal, I know that. Some have run their course, or you've developed different interests or have otherwise grown apart. There is not one thing wrong with ending a relationship that no longer serves you, but if you don't change your own perspective, you're bound to repeat the same old patterns and find yourself right back in the same place. The key is to make changes to your own perspective and thought processes—to build your life and generate happiness instead of looking to change the outside to make you happy on the inside.

I spent many years chasing happiness. As you read in my story, I was constantly changing relationships and locations, trying to find a place that would "make" me happy. It wasn't until I let go of everything and began to learn to be happy right here, right now, with whatever was going on, that I truly regained the power to be happy and free—on purpose and on my own terms. I love the phrase, from a country song I think, "no matter where you go, there you are." If you learn to find the joy and fun and beauty in every place and every person, your happiness will never be stolen away by circumstances.

When you have achieved this level of independent power over your own feelings and perspective, there will still be people you just don't enjoy being around. Unconditional love does not mean that you must spend your time with people who don't align with you, your values, or the way you want to live your life. It's totally okay to choose to love these people from afar. You allow them to make their own choices, withhold judgement, but also make choices for yourself as to who you want to spend your time and energy on. Just because you might be related to someone does not mean that they have to be intricately involved in your life. You choose. We are meant to be diverse and have our own paths AND "birds of a feather flock together." You can choose to have fun hiking with a friend and forgo watching war movies with your brother, all the while loving them both. Real love is bone-deep and voluntary, never born of obligation.

Begin now to change the way you look at people, especially those who are very close to you. Stop criticizing, stop finding fault, stop wishing they would change in any way and learn to appreciate the lovable parts of them and ignore the behaviors that don't please you. Take some really big steps back in your mind and look at your relationships from a broader perspective. When you look back thirty years from now, will laundry on the floor really seem important? Do you really want to squander your energy and happiness by complaining about petty things? Learn to shift your attention away as soon as you notice something that displeases you. Focus instead on what does please you. Be looking always for ways to encourage, praise, and uplift the people you love. If your child puts his plate away one out of ten times, say "Thank you" and "You're wonderful" when he does and when he doesn't, keep your mouth shut. Do this for a week and watch and see if he doesn't start doing the "good" thing way more than before. You're not manipulating or controlling his behavior; this never works. You ARE giving attention and energy to the things you like and letting what you dislike fade away from lack of attention. Your world will absolutely conform to your attention, people included.

ACTION STEPS TO MAKE YOUR RELATIONSHIPS RICHER AND MORE BEAUTIFUL AND LOVING

List of positive aspects.

This is one of my favorite processes from the Abraham Hicks book *Ask and It Is Given*. It's easy and fun and will lift your vibration and brighten your view of anything and anyone. I did this a lot when I was manifesting my dream getaway home. I spent time every day listing all of the things that were wonderful about my apartment and my life. Nothing was too big or small to make it onto the list. If it was pleasing, on the list it went! This process works great with having more loving and happy relationships. Basically, just look at the person and write down everything you can think of that is or has been pleasing to you, no matter how small or large.

Example:
1. I love how you pause and think before answering a question.
2. I love how your eyes crinkle when you laugh.
3. I love that you remembered to take off your muddy shoes at the door yesterday.
4. I love how you smell.
5. I remember when you were a laughing toddler and filled every day with joy.
6. You are a wonderful partner.

You get the idea. If you're thinking of your significant other, you fell in love with them for a reason. Remember that feeling and list all of the positive aspects that drew you to them.

Your children, parents, siblings, friends…All of these people are in your life because you chose them; you saw something you loved and were attracted to and/or wanted to experience. Try to remember those reasons. Look at each of them with the eyes of love, searching for the positive.

"Think and grow rich."

— Napoleon Hill

CHAPTER 17
FOR THE LOVE OF MONEY

In our modern society, money is nearly as necessary to life as your body. Unless you are one of the very few who live in a commune where everyone barters for goods and services, money is the means of exchange by which you get the material things you need and desire. It's also another really good place to begin examining your thoughts, beliefs, and ideas about what it means to be successful and be happy.

Some of the happiest people I have ever seen had no money and barely the basics for survival. Money is not required for happiness, nor does it buy happiness, but that doesn't mean you can't have a rich and loving relationship with money. Your dreams are yours! You might really want a very simple, minimalist life that doesn't require a lot of money. Or you might have dreams of traveling the world first class, building an empire, starting a worldwide charity, or living in a mansion, all of which do require a lot of money. The point is, it's not about the number of zeros in your bank account, it's about the freedom of choice that money brings.

Your beliefs about money are also some of the most deeply ingrained in your subconscious. After all, you started hearing stories about money as soon as you were born, and whether they were stories of abundance or lack you most likely adopted them as your own. And if you're like many people, you later settled into a certain income bracket and found changing that mindset is not an easy task. Studies of lottery winners show that the vast majority go through the money in a very short time; many even go bankrupt. It doesn't matter if they give it away, spend frivolously, or invest poorly—they are returning to the level of abundance they are vibrationally aligned with. Therefore, it is absolutely vital that you make yourself into a vessel that will accommodate the amount of money you want to have.

I can't remind you enough that just like you aren't your body, you're also not your bank account. The amount of money you currently have has nothing to do with your worthiness, divinity, or preciousness in this world. It's simply another form of energy that you can attract or repel, manage or squander. There are many great money mindset teachers out there. John Assaraf and T. Harv Eker are a couple of my favorites. In his book *The Millionaire Mind*, Eker uses the following example to help visualize your relationship with money.

Imagine that you are taking a five-year-old to the ice cream store. He sees a picture of a triple-dip cone and begs for one, so you get it for him. Well, it's huge and cumbersome and he's five, so he promptly drops the whole messy thing. Do you buy him another one? Or do you buy him a single scoop that he is able to manage? The answer is obvious: you buy him the smaller cone. This is how the energy of money works as well. If you don't manage the money you have, the Universe will not give you a larger portion that you haven't shown yourself willing and able to manage.

For most of my life, I had a very easy come, easy go attitude about money; in fact, I was known for saying, "It's only money, we'll make more." I have since really tuned up my attitude about money, and you can see why! If you believe money comes easily, that's great, but believing that it can "go" just as easily...well, that becomes the truth as well. NOT a good money manager attitude. Imagine that you treated your best friends with that same lack of reverence. If you think your best friend is not important, you can take her or leave her, how long is she likely to hang around? The same goes with money. Love it, respect it, manage it, be discerning and aware, but not clinging or desperate, and you'll have a great money love life.

I witnessed a young single mother struggling financially, and even though she knew that her thoughts of lack would attract more lack, she was not able to find her hope and optimism. Her friend threw a fundraiser for her and I helped to get the word out about it on social media, which helped a little. A bit later, she asked me to please share it again and I was about to. Then I realized that this was a great teaching opportunity. I told her that I would be happy to share it again but that it was not going to work as long as she kept her focus on how much she *didn't* have. I encouraged her to try to relax and know that things were going to work out great, that this is a world full of opportunities, that good things were coming. She did this and within the next couple of weeks she had two great job opportunities to choose from and received completely unsolicited assistance to help her bridge the gap. Things looked up VERY quickly once she began focusing on being positive and turning her desperation into hope.

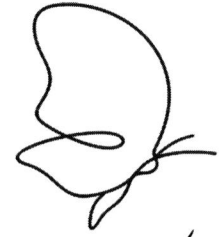

"Have nothing in your home that you don't know to be useful or believe to be beautiful."

- William Morris

CHAPTER 18
LOVING YOUR SPACE AND YOUR DAILY LIFE

NEVER DO ANYTHING YOU DON'T WANT TO DO. I know, you're thinking, *Who WANTS to do the dishes or take out the trash? There are things that MUST be done. If I don't do them, who will?*

You're not wrong, but there is a happier way.

First, let's talk about the difference between inspired action and motivated action. Inspired action feels free and fun and effortless, and gets great results. You are lining up with your purpose and the entire Universe is pitching in to help. You want to do it, you enjoy doing it, and you're excited about what you're creating; you feel great!

Motivation is when you force yourself to do something that you think must be done, using your will or fear of outcomes. When you make yourself do something you don't want to do, your results are subpar and your experience is anything but joyful.

I try to never use the words "motivated" or "productive." In my morning intention-setting, I almost always *intend* to be inspired and inspiring, creative, and effective. Deliberately creating the moments I want ensures that my life unfolds amazingly as I'm choosing to live each day happy and free on purpose.

Here's a great example of how to utilize this fabulous life skill. As of this moment, the first draft of this book is "due" in two days and I still have more than a third of it to write. I wrote most of it on my laptop, but this morning I just couldn't get in the mood to "work." And though this book is a labor of love, aligned with my heart's desire and purpose as a teacher and uplifter, it does count as work and "must be done" if I am to stay true to my path. Now, there were a lot of choices available to me. I could have blown off the whole project. I don't "have to" do anything, including finishing this book. I could have simply procrastinated (I'm a champion procrastinator), or I could have given in to a fear of failure and forced myself to pound out x number of words before allowing myself to do something else more suited to my mood. Instead, I thought, *What if I do something different? What if I light some sweet-smelling candles to warm up the damp gloomy day, and write longhand? Maybe making some cinnamon tea and settling into a comfy spot to write would be fun and feel good.* And it did! I'm so happy right now! I love my fireplace, candles and crystals, and my sweet little cabin with sleeping fur babies everywhere. The words I write feel joyful, flowing, and inspired. I feel like a writer and a teacher and my heart is overflowing. That's what inspired action feels like! Fill your days with inspired action and you'll quickly fall in love with your life.

When you start to form habits of feeling good always, your standards quickly get very high. You become very discerning about how you spend your time and attention. You'll quickly learn to say no to people, thoughts, and actions that steal your joy. You'll learn to distance yourself from negative news and toxic people. And you'll soon notice that when you choose to be happy first…well, the better it gets, the better it gets!

Moments of stress, discomfort, and doubt will be your clues to step way back and get a wider view and a more relaxed state of mind. Moments of intense love, breathtaking joy, and incredible excitement will lead you to laser-like focus, milking the momentum of these great feelings and diluting and dispersing negative thought. You become a master driver, the captain of your ship who honors every part of you, always chooses the happiest course you can see, and has faith that when you move to the edge of the light more light and brighter options will be revealed to you. That's what it means to be happy and free ON PURPOSE: loving this moment and eager to be surprised and enchanted with whatever comes next.

Now, with this new perspective, look at your daily life. How much of your time do you spend doing things that "have to be done" or suffering because they're not? How can you switch things around so that your days are joyful?

Now let's shift to our home and how it factors into the vision of our dream life. We're going to talk a little bit about feng shui here, which is the study of how energy flows in a physical space. There are positive and negative compass directions, in general and for you specifically, based on your birthdate. I've personally found some aspects of feng shui to be a little confusing and contradictory and thus am not called to delve too deeply into it. However, other aspects do speak to me, and can be useful for our discussion. I've also recommended a couple of books and sources in the Resource section in case you're interested in learning more.

Imagine that the world is full of beautiful, free-flowing positive energy (which, in fact, it is). Now imagine that energy flowing into and through your home, filling every corner with bright, sparkling light. Dirt, clutter, and poorly arranged furniture can block the flow of energy, just like it blocks your way when you try to walk through. Remember the woman in the Magic Orchid story? Her home reflected her emotional and energetic state and they changed together. Treat your home with love and reverence and help it to serve you. Organize things so you can always easily find what you want. Have clean sparkling windows to let in beautiful, pure light and positive energy. Create a home that is fit for a queen!

What does this have to do with never doing anything you don't want to do? Figure out ways to enjoy keeping your home clean, lovely, and inviting. If you live with other people, divide up the "chores" according to the most joyful criteria you can come up with; make it a game or other bonding experience. If you don't like it and/or are not good at it, find a way to avoid it if you can. Hire some help!

I like organizing and caring for my things, rearranging furniture, and even cleaning the kitchen and keeping it sparkly. I don't even mind doing light sweeping, but with me and six animals tracking in bits of forest all day, my home requires a lot more than that. I don't enjoy and am not good at big jobs, like cleaning under and behind furniture, washing windows, or cleaning the shower. First I tried finding ways to get better at these big chores; I also tried to find a way to enjoy them. I thought that would be easier than finding someone who was willing to travel to my isolated home and brave my driveway. Eventually I recognized this limiting belief and let it go. I changed my thinking, on purpose, to "There is the perfect person who is willing and able to navigate my driveway, wants the work, and will do a great job for me. And so it is." Sure enough, I found a helper to do the things I don't love, at a price that fits my budget. She does a lot of things to help

Chapter 18 - Loving Your Space And Your Daily Life

me—errands, pet-sitting, and anything else that comes up that I don't want to do or need help with. It's perfect!

If you're thinking you can't "afford" to hire a helper, go back and review the chapter on examining your vocabulary. If it's important to you, you will find the money. Rearrange things, save money from somewhere else, barter your own skills...If you want it then it is yours. You could find a friend who doesn't mind doing windows, in exchange for you organizing her kitchen cabinets. Use your imagination, and in the meantime put it in your vision! There are still many things in my businesses that I am not great at and don't really enjoy, but have not yet found a way to find people to help me within my budget. So "brilliant team" is in my vision! I imagine what it will be like to have marketing and business experts to take care of my website and other business concerns that I don't want to be concerned with.

Never do anything you don't want to do. Life is so much more fun and effective this way!

As I'm reviewing, editing, and revising this book, I have noticed some other things in my life that are not enjoyable and yet are unavoidable, such as cleaning up after a sick dog. I adore my Raki—he is sweet; he is darling; he is my heart. He is also elderly and has a very sensitive digestive system. When he occasionally has diarrhea or vomits in the night, I don't avoid cleaning it up; nor do I know how to enjoy it. I DO, however, know how to make sure it doesn't lower my vibration. I simply do it. I clean up the mess with zero resentment, frustration, or anger. Instead of feeling inconvenienced, I think compassionate thoughts about my sweet dog and how he is feeling. He doesn't want to be sick or make messes. I feel gratitude and love that I still have him around. I am pleased with the environment I've made that makes it easy to clean up (hardwood floors). The point is, even the nastiest, grossest of tasks can't make you unhappy without your permission. Don't give away your power to anything or anyone, especially a pile of poop! Choose your perspective and make "this is no big deal" part of your default vocabulary.

If you're dreaming of a new home or location, really enjoy the dreaming up of the details of that while you make the absolute most of the home you already have. Spend time each morning in your vision of your dream home and the rest of the day looking for positive aspects of the home you have. Add little touches that help you to feel the way you want to feel. Crystals, candles, sweet soft throws for your couch, bright pillows, vases of fresh flowers, plants…The list of little things you can use to add to your joy and enjoyment of your home are endless.

This is a great time to revisit the topic of Magnificent Manifesting Mornings, as it pertains to your daily life. Journal! Your journal is a great place to describe your perfect Tuesday, your perfect Sunday, et cetera. Remember, most people spend more time planning a two-week vacation than they do planning their life. This is due in part because they find it very difficult to get in the habit of daily journaling. If you're one of these people, start small. Every morning, write the date and one thing that is happening. It could be your mood, the moon cycle, the temperature…anything. If you feel like writing more, by all means go for it, but make this small commitment to write just one thing, every single morning. Your journaling practice will grow as you learn to enjoy and relate with it. Just the commitment to start your day on purpose sends a giant signal to the forces that be, and they will all line up to help you to have the kind of day you intend to have.

Meditate! Again, if you're not in this habit, you can start with just five minutes. Sometimes, when I wake up late or have extra activities planned for the morning, I will light one spell candle and set my Insight Timer for ten minutes. Sure, I prefer to have thirty to ninety minutes to journal and plan, light all of my chakra candles, interact with my crystals, do my intention-setting/fire ritual, and study the Tao Te Ching or other current spiritual interest, but if time is short, I still stay committed to my ritual. I take the time, even if it's just ten minutes, to connect with my source and fill myself up with stillness and calm that will serve me all day. I do my very best to live each day on purpose and this practice will serve you as well. Think you can't spare five minutes? Start with one and a half! If you spend thirty seconds journaling and sixty seconds meditating, you've invested just ninety seconds in getting yourself on a path of being a deliberate creator. When you've done that for one week, add a minute; the following week, add another. In thirty weeks, you will have created a habit of deliberate intention-setting/meditating for thirty minutes and your life will feel different. Don't take my word for it, though—prove it to yourself.

PART VI
PUTTING IT ALL TOGETHER

"This above all: to thine own self be true." ~ William Shakespeare

We have covered a lot in this book so far and have really only scratched the surface of ways to create your dream life, on purpose, happy and free. In this section, we'll discuss some frequently encountered obstacles/questions/challenges that may come up for you and some specific techniques to navigate them. Remember, there are no mistakes and there is no failure; there are only steps on your journey, choices that you make in every moment. There is ALWAYS a chance to make a new decision, change your course, reset your outlook and your perspective, be true to who you really are. Everything is a gift! Moments that feel amazing are teaching you how you want your life to feel. Events that hurt your feelings, break your heart, or create doubt or fear are chances to learn, chances to change your viewpoint, grow, and keep becoming. This is a spiral Universe. There is always momentum, and you get to decide which direction that momentum has.

We've all heard the saying "The rich get richer, the poor get poorer." The bible says, "Whoever has will be given more, and they will have an abundance. Whoever does not have, even what they have will be taken from them." Matthew 13:12. There are references to this idea in just about every doctrine.

It simply means that momentum is created and continues until something happens to stop, divert, or reverse it. It's simply physics, and it all starts with your thoughts. Let's say, for example, that you've had an argument with someone. Whenever you think about the argument and how mad you are at the person, you start to have more and more thoughts that feel like that. You rehash how the fight happened and think of all the things you wish you had said, and before you know it you're just as angry (or angrier) than you were during the argument! Another example is when you encounter something unwanted first thing in the morning. Perhaps you notice that your husband drank the last of the coffee and didn't make more. As you notice this, you also notice that he didn't lock the door, left dirty dishes in the sink, and a bunch of other things that piss you off. You start to feel more and more crappy, and the day goes downhill from there. It seems that Murphy's Law reigns and that everything is going wrong. The good news is that you can learn to not only stop this negative spiral, but spin your momentum in the opposite direction. That is one way your strong morning routine serves you.

Here's an example: Let's say you've been suffering with a cold. You wake one morning and instead of mentally complaining about it you notice that you're starting to feel better. You're breathing easier, your body feels lighter, and you feel more rested than you have all week. This is a great first feeling! Then you notice that the sun is shining, which suits your plans for the day perfectly. You hear a slight movement beside you and look at your partner with the feelings of ease and happiness that have already started to flow through you. You feel your heart swell with love and tenderness for this most important person, and that feeling inspires you to slip out of bed and surprise them with their favorite breakfast. As you're doing so you turn on the radio to hear your favorite song playing. You and your partner have fun and happy conversation over breakfast and he happily does the dishes while you visit with him and enjoy your coffee. Your best friend calls and you have a wonderful conversation, your computer beeps with a notification that your online business just made a sale, and so on. Remember, the better it gets the better it gets, or the worse it gets the worse it gets. It all depends on where you are putting your attention and how much power you are giving to circumstances outside yourself.

The beauty of dis-ease, discomfort, problems, obstacles, uncertainties, doubts, fears, and challenges is the contrast they provide. In the above example, this day started out so great because you were DONE with the bad feelings of your cold and the world looks so bright by comparison. When you feel pain or discomfort, say thank you and look for the gifts. This is also a world of opposites. Without darkness there can be no light; sadness and anger are the opposite of joy and love. Male and female, hot and cold, up and down... you get the idea. When you know what you don't like, you can so much more easily decide what you DO like. Clarity feels so amazing. Knowing what you want from life and therefore where to place your attention is the secret to creating amazing spirals of happiness and joy! When you find yourself noticing the unwanted and attracting more of that, make a conscious choice to divert your attention to the pleasing, the wanted, the desirable. You attract what you ARE, so BE in love with every part of your life.

CHAPTER 19
THREE COMMON OBSTACLES AND CHALLENGES

WHAT IF I CAN'T DREAM BIG? WHAT IF I DON'T KNOW WHAT I REALLY WANT?

If these are the questions popping up for you, go back to the Magic Orchard story. Let your basic dream lead the way to bigger, richer, and grander ones.

Unfortunately, this is quite common. As we talked about in the chapter on remembering what you love, we are not encouraged to use our imaginations and we are taught that life has limits. Reframing those beliefs is not as simple as flipping a switch. You are a multifaceted and complicated being. You have many layers that must be peeled away, revealing a different version of yourself with each one. To begin to dream again, start with what you know for sure. You know you want to feel good in your body. Describe that. Imagine what it will feel like when you feel great, the things you'll do, places you'll go, clothes you'll buy. Describe what an everyday moment might feel like. Walking and exploring with ease? Playing with your kids or grandkids? Gardening?

You know you want to be prosperous and have plenty of money, but you have always struggled to have enough. From where you are, you might not even be able to define "plenty of money." What do you know for sure? You know you want to have your daily needs met: shelter, food, clothing, and transportation. What does it feel like to KNOW that there will be no struggle, ever, to keep yourself and your family safe and secure? Savings for unexpected expenses would feel really great also. After these basic needs are met, what are some extra dreams that you might have for your life that will need to be financed? A yearly vacation? Assume that everything you need will be provided for your dream trip—the money, means of transportation, lodging, entertainment, adventure, and exploration. Now what does this dream vacation look and feel like? Where do you want to go? What do you want to experience? How long? What time of year? Do you want to bask in the sunshine on a tropical beach or snuggle up with a hot drink by a fire, surrounded by snowy mountains? Who is with you? Are you traveling alone, with your partner, with your immediate family, extended family, with a large group of friends? Imagine yourself to BE the person who has safety, security, money, confidence, and prosperity, and craft your dream vacation with no attention to how much it will cost. When you are firmly and joyfully in love with the picture you have created in your mind, you can then start to research and figure out what will be needed to make that happen. You might be surprised to find that things you assumed were out of your reach are actually very affordable!

Do you see this progression? You started out not knowing what you want and feeling unable to imagine an amazing life. Now, you have gotten really familiar with the feeling of having all you need AND the opportunity for one special extra thing, your dream vacation. You can picture yourself enjoying this dream vacation in a body that feels great! From this place it will get easier and easier to believe that all things are possible.

You have your motor revving and your creative energy moving in the right direction. Hold onto these feelings, relish them, and watch them grow.

As you practice and exercise your imagination muscles, you will begin to see more and more possibility everywhere you look. You will begin to believe that this awesome Universe has everything you could ever imagine and more. Your soulmate. Your perfect job, career, or business. Beautiful days, weeks, months, and years. Reaching the end of this particular adventure in a human body and knowing that you really lived, joyfully and with no regrets. That you chose to be true to yourself and to create a fantastic experience, in cooperation with a loving Universe.

I'VE TRIED TO MEDITATE BUT I CAN'T QUIET MY MIND.

There is a misconception that you are supposed to stop thought while you're meditating. And if you've tried meditating this way, you've probably noticed that the more you try NOT to think about something, the harder it becomes. What you are really doing during meditation is managing how you *interact* with thought. Instead of trying not to think, just redirect your attention away from those thoughts. This is a positive Universe. There is no such thing as not. "I'm not going to think about this, I'm not going to think about this, I'm not going to think about this" is heard by the Universe as "I'm thinking about this and only this, this has all of my attention." Instead of trying *not* to think or to stop thought, just divert your attention to your breath and how you are *perceiving* your thoughts.

There are three parts of this amazing creature that is you. The real part, who you are at your core, is your soul; your spirit; your inner being. This is the part of you that came from and is a part of God, or Infinite Intelligence, or The Great Spirit—or whatever you call the force that is beating your heart. Like a drop of water is exactly like the ocean from which it came, so are you just like the greatness that created you. This part of you is still and calm and observant. Unflappable. This part of you can see forever in every direction and knows that all is well. This is who you really are.

The second part is your mind. This is the part of your brain that is generating and interpreting the energy of thought. It's always active, always firing off electrical impulses that can be interpreted as thoughts. It interacts with the chemical processes in your body to create emotions and even physical sensations.

The third part is your body. You HAVE a body and a mind. You ARE a divine, eternal spirit, having a short experience in this human body. Your physical self, including your emotions, is a manifestation of your thoughts. You know this. You know that you can simply think of something that angers or shames you and feel your cheeks flush. You can think of something scary and your heart races and your breath catches. Think of the face of a child you love and feel a melting in your heart and an involuntary smile. Your emotions are the absolute most accurate and powerful signaler of what you are thinking and therefore manifesting. That's why it is so important to make feeling good your number one priority.

When you are meditating and the inevitable thoughts come along, use this experience to notice the difference between your mind and your spirit. Your mind is thinking the thoughts, your spirit is observing them. Imagine that you are watching a screen and thoughts are going across it. Choose not to engage, choose to let the images and thoughts just go on by.

Say, "Hi there. I see you but right now I'm choosing to put my attention on my breath. I'm choosing to be at rest and calm and not engaging with specific thoughts." Imagine just letting those thoughts pass on by and remaining undisturbed by their appearance or affected in any way. You're a mildly interested but impartial observer. Just a few minutes of deliberately focusing your attention as you choose will teach you to manage your attention for the rest of the day. You are exercising your "choice" muscles and teaching your brain that it is not the boss of you. This will get easier and easier and feel better and better the more you practice. You will find that you are becoming a being who observes, considers, and responds deliberately, instead of one who is constantly reacting to circumstances or at the mercy of whatever the world puts in your path.

A sacred, daily meditation practice will serve you in every part of your life, I promise. Try it for thirty days and prove it to yourself.

I DON'T HAVE TIME FOR JOURNALING AND MEDITATING

"I don't have time" is one of the most disempowering statements there is. It implies that you are not in charge of your life or the exact twenty-four hours you have each day. The truth is you have time for anything that is important to you. If you think you don't have time to get aligned with who you really are and to create your days on purpose, you are making a choice. You're choosing not to give attention to learning to create your life on purpose. So the true statement is, "I'm *choosing not to make time* for these activities." First thing, take back your power. Change your words with the intent of changing what you think and how you feel.

Now consider this. What if you spent thirty minutes each

morning getting focused and aligned, putting yourself firmly in the driver's seat of your life, and the result is that everything else, all day, is easier and more joyful? What if you find that your daily activities get easier and shorter? What if you find that things that "must be" done are inexplicably completed by someone else or for some reason become unnecessary? What if you find that getting aligned and taking care of yourself magically seems to add hours of free time to your day?

Now I turn again to the Abraham Hicks book, *Ask and it is Given* and a wonderful process called the "place mat process." It's a great way to begin to feel like you are in charge of your "list" instead of your list being in charge of you. You can read the specific process in the book if you wish, but basically you create two columns on a large piece of paper. One column is for you. Write here the things that you absolutely plan to, want to, and will do today. The second column is assigned to the Universe. EVERYTHING else on your to-do list goes here. Feel really good and relaxed about how much you have assigned to yourself for today and have total faith that a loving and resourceful Universe will take care of everything else. Then let it go. In Esther Hick's version she actually threw the list away, knowing that she had been heard, that Source was on the job and she need not give it another thought.

The result is that you'll find those tasks assigned to the Universe completed by someone else, suddenly becoming not necessary, or taken care of in any number of ways. Perhaps there's a phone call you need to make, but instead the person calls you or sends an email that resolves everything. Your husband is inspired to wash the car; your daughter is inspired to fold the laundry. The Universe has unlimited resources and endless possibilities for ways to help you, if you just get out of the way.

    The remainder of this book is a study guide, a checklist if you will, to help you embed these habits of being and thinking into your very soul. You're beginning to really feel your power and witness how the world changes according to your attention to it. You are aware of the words you think and say, how you relate to your body, your family, and the world. My wish for you is that you understand that learning to be totally in love with your life in this moment and excited about what is to come is the perfect place to BE. And all you need do is decide. Decide that this is your new reality, that life is good and getting better, and you're the one manifesting every single thing. Stay with it! Practice the skills in this book and make up some of your own. Share! Let your light be an inspiration to everyone who sees you. Love your life. Choose Happiness and Freedom! On Purpose!

CHAPTER 20
STUDY AND PRACTICE GUIDE

If you are a life coach or personal development teacher of any kind, you can use *Happy and Free on Purpose* to lead your students or clients down a path of learning to create their best life. You might also go through this with your friends in a book club. Either way, use this study and implementation guide to structure your journey.

Ritualize it! In nearly every chapter of this book there are suggestions on creating rituals to add reverence and meaning to all parts of your life. Add some wine, food, tea, games, and prizes to your study and really uplevel the fun and progress. Choose to do these activities together so as to inspire and support each other and create amazing relationships among your group. Have fun with this! Life is supposed to be fun. It's supposed to be rich, varied, and interesting. You're supposed to feel all levels of emotion: contentment, satisfaction, high-flying joy, love, and appreciation. You have everything you need to live in happiness and freedom every single day, on your way to greater and greater joy. These processes will add momentum to your journey.

Each activity corresponds with a chapter in the book, so use the chapters as a guide and for inspiration as you complete each of these explorations and activities. Love yourself! Love each other! Love your journal and the masterpiece of a life that you are beginning right now to create.

IMPLEMENTATION AND STEPS

1. Get a journal! There is no more powerful tool to help you to stay connected with your intentions and to help you learn to be a deliberate creator of your life. (Chapter 1)
2. Read the whole book and make notes in your journal.
3. Get ready to get ready! Begin or recommit to a daily practice of self-awareness and mindfulness. Pay attention to the thoughts that come up throughout your day, the beliefs that reveal themselves, and the words you speak. (Chapters 3-4)
4. Make a list of everything that is wonderful about your life right now in each of the following areas. Make a separate list for each area. (Chapter 5)
    a. Body/Health
    b. Money/Financial Health
    c. Relationships
    d. Career/Work
    e. Home
    f. Lifestyle
5. Enter your starting point. Describe what you would like to improve in each area of your life in the following areas, but don't spend too much time here! Remember, knowing what you don't want will help you to have clarity about what you DO want, which is where you will place your attention from here on. Just examine the gifts in your current circumstances

and learn what you can from them. (Chapter 6)

    a. Body/Health
    b. Money/Career/Work
    c. Relationships
    d. Lifestyle

6. Make a list of everything you have ever loved to do that you don't do anymore. As far back as you can remember, list activities that brought you joy. (Chapter 7)

7. Make a list of wishes unfulfilled—everything you would love to see, do, and experience. (Chapter 8)

8. Make a list of your values, choose the top five, and rank them in order of importance. (Chapter 9)

9. Make a list of your talents, skills, accomplishments, awards, and achievements. (Chapter 10)

10. Make a list of your passions. (Chapter 11)

11. Write your new story. Project yourself out into your future; it could be one year, ten years, thirty years, or whatever time period that feels best to you. Now, write the story of your life when your dreams are fulfilled. Use the following guidelines. (Chapter 12)

    a. Written in the present tense
    b. Bathed in gratitude and appreciation
    c. Written in the positive
    d. Full of emotion and color
    e. Open-ended so the Universe has room to improve on your vision

12. Test your dream story to make sure it's a dream worthy of YOU! (Chapter 13)

a. Does reading my vision make me feel alive and excited?
b. Do I need help from my source (higher power) to create this life?
c. Does my new story require me to grow?
d. Is there good to be created for others and the world?

13. Create a morning ritual. Gather tools to help you start the first moment of your day in joy, love, and appreciation. (Chapter 14)

14. Create your morning *spiritual* ritual (Chapter 14)

    a. Gather tools to use in your ritual (i.e. a journal, candles, incense, essential oils, colored pens, paper, and fireproof vessel (cauldron))
    b. Create your morning spiritual ritual. Decide when, where, and how long your ritual will be and what it will look and feel like.
    c. Plan for journaling. Make reminder notes in your journal to try these entries: Magic Orchid, I AM statements, I AM creating statements, and highlights of your dream story.
    d. Plan for meditation. Download Insight Timer or decide what tools you will use.
    e. Make a promise to yourself (and a pact with your group if you like) to commit to creating Magnificent Manifesting Mornings.

15. Create an amazing relationship with your body. (Chapter 15)

    a. Make a list of positive aspects of your body (at least twenty-one items)

- b. Create reminders to love yourself (i.e. affirmations printed and posted in your shower, notes on your mirrors, etc.)
- c. Start a written conversation with your body in which you ask it what your body is feeling and what it needs.
- d. Make a list of possible actions that might feel good, be fun, and move you in the direction of your perfect health and vitality.

16. Create a loving and fun relationship with food. (Chapter 15)

    a. Keep a food journal for a week (or more) to learn what food choices you are making and why and how your body responds.
    b. Create at least one ritual per month that involves food and includes joy and fun.
    c. Create a mindfulness ritual to use at every meal.

17. Create a great attitude and relationship with sleep. (Chapter 15)

    a. Write down your current beliefs and experiences with sleep and ask yourself if these beliefs serve you.
    b. Create bedtime rituals.
    c. Experiment with different bedtimes and napping.

18. Get in tune with the kind of movement your body wants and loves. (Chapter 15)

    a. Examine and write down your current beliefs about exercise.

b. Make a list of things to try doing or NOT doing to feel better in your body.

c. Create one monthly ritual that includes moving your body.

19. Learn to be aware, reverent, deliberate, and appreciative of your breath. (Chapter 15)

    a. Create a daily ritual for connecting with your breath (meditation).

    b. Set reminders to stop and breathe intentionally throughout your day.

20. Fall back in love with love and the people you share your life with. (Chapter 16)

    a. Honestly examine, write about, and share how invested you are in the lives of others.

    b. Make lists of positive aspects for each of the people who play an important role in your life.

    c. Create at least one monthly ritual that allows you to deepen your connection with the people in your life—as a family, one-on-one, or both.

21. Love up on your money! (Chapter 17)

    a. Examine, write, and share your beliefs about money and wealth.

    b. Make a "gratitude" list for all that you have and all the ways you are prosperous.

    c. Write some statements around money and your current and future prosperity that feel good to you.

22. Fall in love with your home and your daily life. (Chap-

ter 18)

- a. Review your dream life and add details of the home you would really love!
- b. Review your dream life and journal your perfect everyday.
- c. Journal about one special event that you would love to have in your life each year.
- d. Make a list of positive aspects about your daily life as it is now.
- e. Make a list of all the things on your to-do list that you really don't want to do and begin imagining ways of getting out of them or making them fun.

23. CELEBRATE! You now know so much more about yourself and your dreams! You have a fully stocked toolbox for living each day as you choose, happy and free on purpose! You see the value of feeling great and set very high standards for how you spend your time and where you direct your attention. If you stay on this path, changing course as you learn and grow, always choosing happiness and freedom, you will soon be so in love with your life that you're bursting with it! And your joy will shine on everyone you meet.

RESOURCES

The Art and Truth of Transformation for Women (2020), Powerful You Publishing. https://www.amazon.com/dp/B08JWTFH2G

Brené' Brown. (2018). *Dare to Lead. Brave Work. Tough Conversations. Whole Hearts.* https://amzn.to/3rK5CQu

Mary Morrissey – Life Mastery Institute

Don Miguel Ruiz. (1997). *The Four Agreements: A Practical Guide to Personal Freedom (A Toltec Wisdom Book).* Amber-Allen Publishing.

Karen Flaherty. (2018), *Getting to Know YOU: Embrace Your Unique Blueprint to Make Decisions You Love and Trust – A Human Design Guidebook.* Custom Health Solutions, LLC. https://www.amazon.com/dp/B07HB8PRHK

Dr. Wayne Dyer. (2009). *Change your Thoughts, Change Your Life: Living the Wisdom of the Tao.* Hay House. https://www.amazon.com/dp/140191750X

Jamie Della. (2019). *The Book of Spells: The Magic of Witchcraft.* Ten Speed Press.

Aurora Kane. (2020). *A Handbook of Lunar Cycles, Lore, and Mystical Energies (Mystical Handbook).* Wellfleet Press.

Dr. Joe Dispenza. (2017). *Becoming Supernatural: How Common People are Doing the Uncommon.* Hay House.

Esther and Jerry Hicks. (2004). *Ask and it is Given: Learning to Manifest Your Desires.* Hay House.

Craig Hamilton (June 1, 2020). "Rethinking Meditation: The Miraculous Practice of Direct Awakening." https://craighamiltonglobal.com/rethinking-meditation-the-miraculous-practice-of-direct-awakening/

John Assaraf. (2007). *Having it All: Achieving Your Life's Goals and Dreams.* Atria Books.

T. Harv Eker. (2005). *Secrets of The Millionaire Mind: Mastering the Inner Game of Wealth.* Harper Business.

Louise Hay. (2016). *Mirror Work: 21 Days to Heal Your Life.* Hay House.

Mark Sisson (2012). The Primal Blueprint: Reprogram you genes for effortless weightloss, vibrant health, and boundless energy. Primal Nutrition, Inc. https://amzn.to/3rJ9XDl

Mark Sisson. (2011). *The Primal Blueprint 21-Day Total Body Transformation: A step-by-step, gene reprogramming action plan.* Primal Nutrition, Inc. https://amzn.to/2OP32KJ

Lauren G. Foster. (Host). The How to Choose Happiness and Freedom Show. "Satu Chantal Pitkamaki - Breathe Light for Happiness and Health." www.behappyfirst.org/57

davidji. (2017). *Secrets of Meditation: A Practical Guide to Inner Peace and Personal Transformation, Revised Edition.* Hay House. https://amzn.to/3tj8V1G.

Karen Rauch Carter. (2000). *Move Your Stuff, Change Your Life: How to use Feng Shui to Get Love, Money, Respect, and Happiness.* Simon & Shuster.

FAVORITE JOURNALS

The LANG Companies Flight Spiral Journal (traditional journal size – 240 pages) https://amzn.to/3qM5ezD

Studio Oh! Hardcover Journal, "Live in the Moment" design (notebook size – 160 pages) https://amzn.to/3rJw7FZ

MEDITATION SOCIAL APP

Insight Timer. https://insighttimer.com/

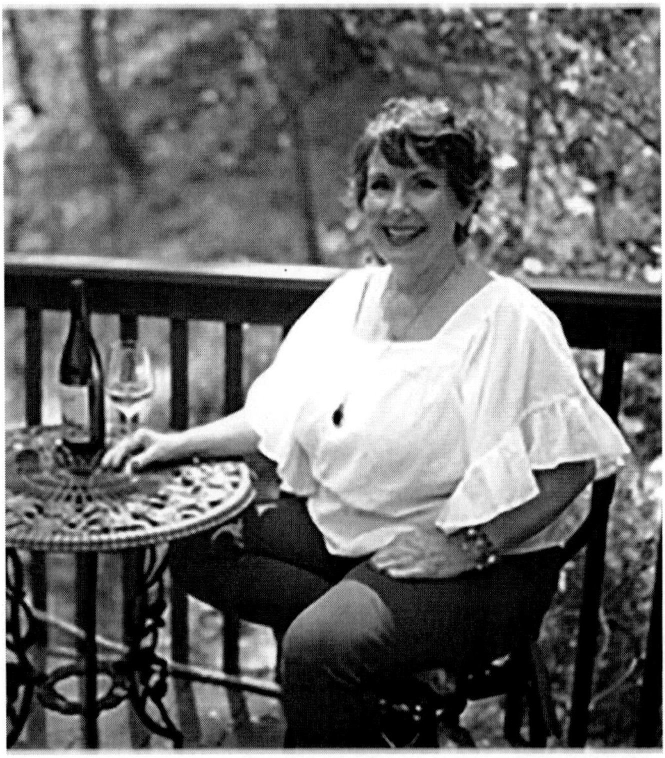

NOTE FROM THE AUTHOR

I am so honored and blessed to be chosen to play a small part in your personal growth, in your process of learning to claim the happiness that is your birthright. Thank you for being here!

When you read my story in this book, you will see that I was once just like you. Trying everything to find happiness, success, and fulfillment and always falling short. I'm STILL reaching for more happiness; the difference is that now, I'm in love with my present moments, right where I am and I'm totally jazzed about the new dreams that are coming true for me. I'm no longer "seeking" happiness. I'm creating it, choosing it, allowing it, living into all the beauty I can find. As you read these words, you are helping make one of my dreams come true! Your dreams can come true too, sooner than you think!

Visit me on line and become a part of the Be Happy First Tribe. Send me an email with your questions and your stories. You are a light to everyone who sees you and you can begin to shine brighter and brighter every day. I'm thrilled to help you along this path.

My Mission is to help 1 million women step into their

power to create amazing lives, on their own terms. Happy and Free on Purpose, before my 60th birthday in 2025. You are MEANT to be happy, healthy, wealthy, loved, and free, in love with your life and in love with where you're going. Thank you for being a part of this mission! Keep shining!

Lauren

Website: www.laurengfoster.com
Email Lauren@laurengfoster.com